THE SILK
ROADS

THE SILK ROADS

A History of the Great Trading Routes Between East and West

GEORDIE TORR

— PICTURE CREDITS —

Bridgeman Images: 30, 41, 58, 63, 76, 106, 125, 128, 137, 143, 167, 168, 174, 182, 184, 198, 201, 202, 204, 206, 214, 218

David Woodroffe: 8, 21, 67, 233

Getty Images: 78, 96, 251

Mary Evans Picture Library: 109

Metropolitan Museum of Art: 19, 110

Shutterstock: 11, 13, 16, 23, 25, 32, 36, 38, 52, 71, 84, 90, 114, 117, 124, 133, 149, 152, 153, 160, 165, 177, 187, 189, 207, 236, 238, 241, 247

Wikimedia Commons: 39, 44, 46, 47, 61, 69, 88, 93, 101, 103, 112, 122, 135, 140, 141, 146, 157, 158, 166, 172, 180, 192, 196, 209, 223, 224, 227, 228, 230

This edition published in 2021 by Arcturus Publishing Limited
26/27 Bickels Yard, 151–153 Bermondsey Street,
London SE1 3HA

AD007735UK

Printed in the UK

MIX
Paper from responsible sources
FSC
www.fsc.org
FSC® C020471

CONTENTS

INTRODUCTION

The Silk Road was arguably the most important thoroughfare in human history. Wars were waged over it and desperate diplomacy employed to keep it open. Trod by countless merchants and missionaries, envoys and bandits, emperors, kings, princesses and peasants, it brought both prosperity and disaster, providing a conduit for the trade in luxury goods, the movement of marauding armies and the transmission of devastating diseases. But perhaps most importantly, it was also an artery for ideas, a driving force in the exchange of culture and technology across Eurasia; primarily running east–west between China and the Middle East, its impact extended even further afield.

Only coined during the late 19th century, the term Silk Road is a misnomer in more ways than one. First, it wasn't a single 'road' but an ever-changing network of routes, often barely discernible tracks through inhospitable regions – hardly deserving of the name road. Second, although the Roman Empire's desire for Chinese silk provided much of the early impetus for trade along the network, the routes carried much more, from spices, incense and gems to horses, porcelain and weapons. And finally, the overland routes were connected to, and eventually replaced by, a maritime Silk Road that linked ports around the margins of the Indian Ocean and through to the Mediterranean.

In telling the story of the Silk Road, the focus is sometimes on its heartland in Central Asia and Chinese Turkestan – the area around the Taklamakan Desert and Pamir Mountains. In other contexts,

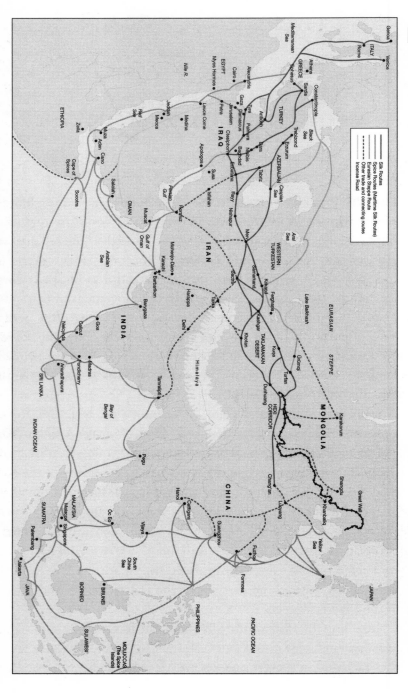

A map showing the various routes of the old Silk Roads on land and by sea.

it becomes relevant to encompass a much broader swathe across Eurasia from the shores of the Mediterranean to the East China Sea, and to look in more detail at the Middle East and central China, even India or Siberia. This book reflects that fluidity, shifting its gaze according to the aspect under consideration.

The Silk Road's existence is a consequence of both humanity's propensity for mercantilism and the geography of Central Asia, with its formidable mix of mountains and deserts, which constrained the options available for east–west trade. Millennia in the making, the highway entered its golden age towards the end of the first millennium CE during China's Tang dynasty, but eventually faded from memory as traders turned to less arduous routes and the desert sands obscured and then obliterated the ancient camel tracks.

Since they were rediscovered during the 19th century, the legendary trade routes of the overland Silk Road have captured the popular imagination, conjuring up images of parched deserts, fertile valleys and treacherous mountain passes, isolated oasis settlements and imperial cities, vast camel caravans, nomad armies and lone pilgrims. And with the opening up of Central Asia following the dissolution of the Soviet Union, Silk Road tourism is on the cusp of a boom.

In the 21st century, as the world becomes increasingly interconnected, the Silk Roads have taken on a new lease of life. Their heritage value has been acknowledged by the United Nations, new rail links have already been established, and China is embarking on an ambitious (and costly) plan to reopen multiple strands of the ancient routes – the beginning of a new chapter in one of history's greatest stories.

— I —
ORIGINS
OF THE
SILK ROAD

The vast territory through which the various branches of the Silk Road and its predecessors ran includes a wide diversity of habitats, from forbidding deserts and extensive grasslands to high mountain ranges and their foothills. Chill northern forests give way to semi-arid steppe, which in turn morphs into the deserts of Central Asia: the Taklamakan, the Gobi, the Karakum, the Kyzylkum.

PHYSICAL GEOGRAPHY

Mountain ranges dissect the region: the Altai, the Pamirs, the Tian Shan, the Karakoram, the Kunlun. Rising to elevations of up to 4,000 m (13,000 ft), these formidable peaks create what were, in the early part of their human history, a series of essentially self-contained areas. Far from any ocean and its moist winds, they receive scant rainfall: standing water is generally scarce, although there are some lakes, rivers and small spring-fed oases. The lack of water for agriculture constrained settlement, as only rivers flowing from the mountains provided predictable supplies.

This combination of forbidding mountain ranges, harsh deserts and a general lack of resources, in particular water, limited the options not only for the formation of settlements in Central Asia but also for routes connecting those settlements. Diversity of landscapes and climates meant that cultural development across the continent was diverse too, in both its speed and pathways. Thus physical geography shaped the Silk Roads.

The geography of the Silk Road encompassed massive mountain ranges such as the Altai in western Siberia and northwest Mongolia.

HUMAN GEOGRAPHY

Modern humans probably began to move into Eurasia about 40,000 years ago. These early hunter-gatherers were then slowly replaced from around 9000BCE as migrants arrived from the Middle East, bringing with them knowledge of primitive farming.

However, the northern steppe regions proved inhospitable to farmers. The climatic conditions – low, unpredictable rainfall and high evaporation rates – and infertility of the soils, combined with the low levels of agricultural technology at the time, made farming difficult, if not impossible. Yet the steppe has one thing in abundance: grass. And not just any old grass, but highly nutritious grass. Thus it provided perfect conditions for the development of livestock herding. Over time, the geographical differences between the northern and southern regions meant the northern areas were mostly populated by nomadic herders, while in the south lived settled farmers, although it was by no means a clear-cut distinction.

— TIMELINE —

C. 4500BCE *Beginning of the Copper Age*

C. 3500BCE *Domestication of the horse and the Bactrian camel; horse-based pastoralism in the Eurasian steppe*

C. 3300BCE *Beginning of the Bronze Age*

C. 3000BCE *Wheeled transport develops*

C. 2000BCE *Steppe Route and Nephrite and Lazurite roads in operation*

C. 1800BCE *Settlements begin to form in the south; nomadic pastoralism develops in the north*

C. 1300BCE *Development of horse-based warfare*

C. 1046BCE *Start of Zhou dynasty*

C. 1000BCE *Nomadism spreads across the steppe; horse-based warfare becomes more common*

C. 900BCE *Nomads begin to attack settled farming communities*

C. 600BCE *Horseback riding spreads across the steppe*

550BCE *Start of Persian (Achaemenid) Empire*

C. 500BCE *Persian Royal Road completed*

C. 400BCE *Archery and riding combined, cavalries emerge*

336BCE *Alexander becomes king of Macedonia at the age of 20*

330BCE *Alexander the Great defeats the Achaemenids*

323BCE *Alexander the Great dies*

312BCE *Start of Seleucid Empire*

250BCE *Start of Bactrian Kingdom*

247BCE *Start of the Parthian Empire*

221BCE *Qin dynasty unites China*

Those northern steppes saw one of the most significant innovations in human history, when, in around 3500BCE, steppe livestock herders (in what is now northern Kazakhstan) discovered how to domesticate the horse. From there, the knowledge spread to more settled groups in Turkmenistan over the next 500 years or so. Domestication of the Bactrian camel is thought to have taken place at around the same time, probably in what is now southern Russia. By the third to second millennium BCE, camels were widely used as draught animals. Livestock domestication brought beasts of burden for carrying agricultural products and trade goods; they could also be used for transportation, for meat and as weapons of war.

The next important innovation was wheeled transport, thought to have developed in western Asia towards the end of the fourth millennium BCE and spread into Central Asia during the first half of the third millennium BCE. Its first appearance in the steppe regions has been dated to the latter half of the third millennium BCE. In southern Turkmenistan during the Late Bronze Age, towards the

Domesticated Bactrian camels were used for transporting goods not only across inhospitable deserts but also over high mountains and cold steppes.

end of the second millennium BCE, there was a series of further innovations, most notably the invention of the spoked wheel, and hence production of lighter vehicles, including horse-drawn chariots, which became important for warfare.

The use of wheeled transport significantly boosted productivity, enabling farmers to bring in crops more easily and livestock herders to follow their cattle, sheep and goats to new pastures. This in turn fostered the development of nomadic pastoralism, which would become the dominant way of life across the Eurasian steppe. Demographic pressures within agricultural societies probably also contributed to migration and the transition to a nomadic existence by forcing the more fragile groups living on the edges of farming areas to travel in search of better conditions.

Perhaps more importantly for the development of the Silk Road, wheeled transport meant, too, that people could travel greater distances, and thus came into contact with more people. This would have fostered greater cultural contact between remote regions, in turn promoting trade. Light chariots also allowed movement of significant quantities of raw materials; a text from about 1800BCE discovered in the ancient city of Ur in southern Mesopotamia refers to a single shipment of copper that weighed 20 tonnes.

As human populations grew, so did the need for food, and hence also livestock herds. Overgrazing became a problem and communities were typically forced to move several dozen kilometres to new, ungrazed pastures every 20 years or so. The nomads also practised transhumance, moving seasonally several times a year between different pastures at different altitudes. Interestingly, many of the routes taken by Silk Road traders match those used by early nomadic livestock herders.

With the establishment of mobile livestock herding, pastoral peoples were able to make long-distance migrations. Loosely organized cultural communities formed across vast territories, interacting with each other, trading goods and occasionally attacking more settled groups in the south. Their contacts and influence extended over large areas, along with the military culture necessary to protect herds and conquer new territories.

A mobile livestock economy also meant that herd animals became commodities that could be traded, but could also be stolen. This was more than likely one of the factors that led to the construction of settlements with defensive walls. And with migration came competition, as groups began to vie for control over limited resources, and conflict became more frequent – another reason why settlements began to need defences.

Global climate undergoes irregular cycles of warming and cooling. As humans were spreading out across Eurasia, these cycles brought periods when the climate became more favourable for farming and herding, increased warmth and rainfall causing the steppe grasslands to become more verdant and crops more productive. These warmer periods often coincided with episodes of conquest, nomads banding together to invade settled areas. During cooler periods, farming and herding both became more marginal and humans were compelled either to migrate to regions where conditions were more benign or to innovate in some way.

Overall, this link between climate and human demography is a key factor in the evolution of the Silk Road. By forcing or inducing nomads to move, the changing climate created conditions for intensification of cultural contact and exchange.

Another significant innovation was the discovery of metal production. The steppe became a key centre for copper after rich deposits were discovered in the Ural Mountains. By the beginning of the third millennium BCE, copper mines were active not far from the Kargaly deposit in the southern Urals, which was among the richest known. Development of smelting techniques then made metal more common, while the creation of alloys such as bronze, brass or steel led to an increase in quality and durability of metal implements.

All this resulted in the birth of a new culture, living in fortresses and engaging in chariot warfare, probably to protect the mines, the metallurgists themselves and their products, not to mention livestock. In the south, this combination of fortified settlements and advanced metallurgy meant the development of towns. However, environmental conditions on the steppe weren't suited to such settlements, and this mode of living was largely abandoned. By the 18th century BCE, as urbanization was taking off, it was largely abandoned on the steppe in favour of extensive livestock husbandry over large areas of land.

During the 12th to eighth centuries BCE, on the lowland plains of Central Asia, fertile valleys became centres of civilization as large populations formed, with grand walled citadels at their centre and smaller settlements clustered at the periphery. The people in these settlements started out mostly as livestock herders, but gradually shifted to farming. Irrigation systems became more sophisticated,

A copper ore quarry in Bashkortostan, Sibai, Russia, located in the Eurasian steppe territory. Since the third millennium BCE, this area has been the site of copper mining, although conditions are less than ideal as a place for human settlement.

their construction and maintenance increasingly requiring significant effort by organized collective labour.

These more complex, settled societies thus began to consume labour (often in the form of slaves) and commodities, including raw materials for building, weapons for defence and territorial expansion, and luxuries for the elite on a large scale. The demand for such commodities fuelled trade. Economic prosperity also brought further social complexity, with more structured hierarchies and clearer divisions of power and labour. Thus two of the prime movers behind the development of trade networks across Eurasia were demand for commodities by settled peoples and mobility of the steppe pastoralists.

The growth of settlements led to the emergence of a centralized authority – a ruler. And rulers need, or at least desire, 'precious things' as a visible signal that sets them apart from everyone else – the ruled. And so the creation of a ruling class creates a market for items that are valuable purely on the basis of beauty or rarity, rather than utility, another important driver of trade. As early as the second millennium BCE, communities in Mesopotamia had become avid consumers of a wide range of commodities that could only be sourced beyond its borders. This demand for what were often luxury items, driven by successive aspirational elites, created a large, lucrative market that relied on ever-expanding trading networks spreading deep into the surrounding regions.

THE STEPPE ROUTE

One of the most significant precursors to the Silk Road was an ancient overland route through the Eurasian steppe. Extending for some 10,000 km (6,200 miles), it ranged about 10° north and south of latitude 40°N, connecting eastern Europe to northeastern China via what is now Mongolia, from the mouth of the Danube River to the Pacific Ocean. To the north it was bounded by the taiga forests of what is now Russia, to the south by semi-deserts and deserts.

During the third and second millennia BCE, the population of Eurasia went through a period of flux, with large shifts of people over a wide area, creating a complex pattern of migratory movements, transformations and cultural interactions. Eventually, regional networks were established among settlements, leading to a remarkable degree of social interconnectedness. This led to trade, in both goods and ideas, and to the creation of what became known as the Steppe Route.

Trade along the route, which was primarily based around silk and horses but also took in furs, weapons, musical instruments, semi-precious stones and jewels, and metals and metal objects, began at least 2,000 years before the classical Silk Road. Turquoise and tin travelled from Central Asia, lapis lazuli and gold from Afghanistan, carnelian from India, and copper from the Urals.

Perhaps the most important trade was in minerals, as stones were transported from a few mining sites to settlements some distance away. The mountains of Central Asia contain a number of semi-precious minerals such as lazurite, nephrite (jade), carnelian and turquoise, and trade in these fuelled trade in the region.

Around the end of the third millennium BCE, jade/nephrite quarried in Khotan and Yarkand (in what would later be known as Chinese Turkestan) was being sold in northern China, where it was in use by the time of the Longshan culture and was particularly evident in the Zhou dynasty. The route taken by this trade has been described as the 'Nephrite Road'. Similarly, there was a 'Lazurite Way' via which lapis lazuli mined in Sar-e-Sang in what is now Badaghshan province in eastern Afghanistan was transported to Iran, Mesopotamia and even Egypt, and carnelian from Sogdiana (modern Uzbekistan/Tajikistan, centred on Samarkand) and Bactria (modern northern Afghanistan, centred on Balkh) was taken to western Asia, along with turquoise from Khoresm (near the Aral Sea).

Given the distances involved, it seems unlikely that many people travelled the length of the Steppe Route. Rather, it was a trade route along which goods travelled, mostly passed from one short-distance

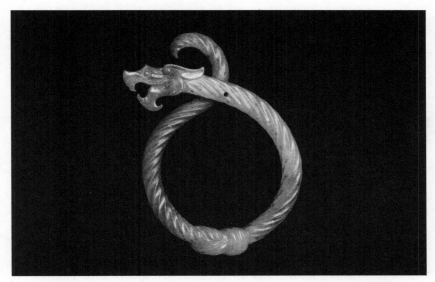

A knotted dragon pendant made of jade from the Eastern Zhou dynasty (475–221BCE) is typical of the ornate luxury goods that fuelled trade along the Silk Road.

trader to the next, or simply from one pastoralist community to the next. Much of it would likely have relied on small horse, donkey and camel caravans, but maritime trade would also have linked settlements in the Persian Gulf, Arabia and India.

THE PERSIAN ROYAL ROAD

Early roads in Central Asia were most likely established by the Hittite civilization and other kingdoms in western Anatolia (modern Turkey) during the second millennium BCE, for a mixture of commercial, political and military purposes. However, the first network that could be called a true precursor to the Silk Road was what became known as the Persian Royal Road, completed in around 500BCE.

This was built to allow access to, and administration of, conquered cities across the Persian Empire. The greatest empire the world had yet seen took up more than five million sq km (two million sq miles) of territory, stretching east to west for about 5,000 km (3,100 miles), from the Indus River to the Black Sea and south to the coast of North Africa, and containing dozens of formerly independent states. It's thought that as much as a fifth of the global population lived within its borders – some 70–80 million people.

The Royal Road was almost certainly built largely over existing roads constructed by the Hittites and their successors, the Assyrians. The Assyrians were already trading with Kaneš (in modern Turkey) by the early second millennium BCE and it's likely that the route from Assyria to the west was well established by the beginning of the Persian age. Darius I, king of the Persian Achaemenid Empire from 522BCE, improved and extended these roads into the network.

The Persians' main road connected one of the four capitals of their empire, Susa (Shush in present-day Iran) in the Lower Zagros Mountains, about 250 km (150 miles) east of the Tigris River, to the city of Sardis (Sart in present-day Turkey), capital of the ancient kingdom of Lydia in the volatile region of Asia Minor, about 100 km (60 miles) east of the port of Smyrna (modern Izmir) on the Aegean Sea. Covering a distance of more than 2,850 km (1,770 miles), it took in the cities of Kirkuk, Nineveh, Edessa and Hattusa, the capital of the Hittite Empire.

While the exact route is unknown, it would have crossed the central plains of what is now Turkey. One branch, from Fars to Sardis, crossed the foothills of the Zagros Mountains and then headed east of the Tigris and Euphrates rivers, through Kilikia and Cappadocia before reaching Sardis. Another ran from Sardis to Cappadocia and Cilicia before passing into Armenia and then down to Arbela, crossing the Tigris and finally reaching Susa.

From Susa, the road continued on through the formidable Persian Gate to Persepolis, the ceremonial capital of the Achaemenid Empire, a 552-km (343-mile) journey made up of 23 stages. It intersected with a number of other road systems that eventually reached the ancient kingdoms of Media (northwestern Iran), Bactria

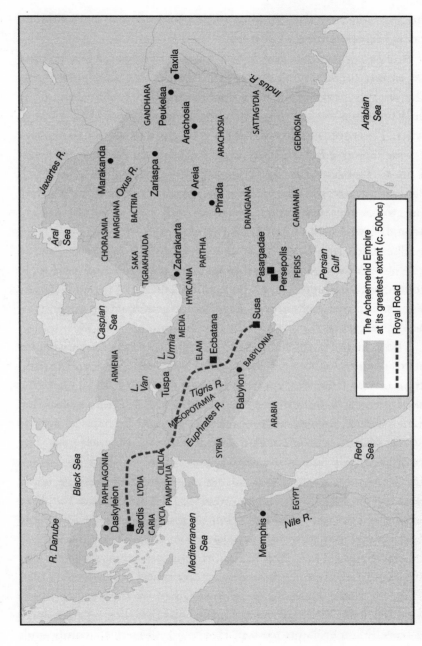

This map shows the route connecting Susa and Sardis around 500BCE, at the height of the Achaemenid Empire.

and Sogdiana as well as crossing south into the Indian subcontinent, across Mesopotamia and into Egypt.

It didn't follow the most logical route – neither the shortest nor the easiest – connecting the major cities of the Persian Empire. The shortest way would have been from Susa to Babylon, along the Euphrates to the capital of Cilicia, Tarsus, and from there to Lydia. This route would also have passed close to the ocean, making it more effective for trade. Instead, the road ran through the heart of the ancient Assyrian Empire, so many archaeologists believe that the westernmost sections may have originally been built by Assyrian kings to connect their capital, Nineveh, with Susa, while also passing through towns such as Arbela and Opis.

The road's significance was underlined by the resources used to protect it. A total of 111 guard posts were scattered along the main section, with frequent patrols helping to reduce the threat posed by bandits, and many of the side roads were protected by outposts of the Persian army.

These guard posts also served as relay stations for messengers called chapars, who carried missives between Susa and Sardis. Stone tablets from Persepolis describe a system of horse changing called pirradaziš. Guard posts had stables with fresh horses so that when a chapar arrived with a message, it could be handed over to another chapar, who set out on a fresh horse for the next post. The previous chapar and horse would then return to their post when they were sufficiently rested. Using this system, a message could travel the length of the road in a week or two, rather than the three months that it would take a traveller on foot. This allowed for rapid communication of news and proclamations to and from the king.

Guard posts were often set up at river crossings and near city gates, but many were, by necessity, in desert and other barren areas. While the posts' locations were constrained by the need to be no more than a day's ride apart, a side effect was that they created places for travelling merchants to stop. Hence caravanserais – compounds for accommodating trade caravans – often grew up around them.

Persepolis was the ceremonial capital of the Achaemenid Empire around 515BCE. It was a monumental centre designed to reinforce the Persian kings' power and rule, and is located 60 km (40 miles) northeast of Shiraz in modern Iran.

The existence of these protected caravanserais ensured that even after the fall of the Persian Empire, the Royal Road continued to be used by merchants and traders, and would eventually come to serve as one of the Silk Road's main arteries.

As the Royal Road was built along routes of even older roads and paths, determining its composition has been difficult. However, there are some surviving sections that date from Darius' time at Gordion and Sardis. In these areas, the road was about 6 m (20 ft) wide, built as a cobble pavement over a low embankment. In some places it was faced with a curb made from dressed stone. However, it's thought that most of the road was made of packed earth, was wide enough to support the movement of mobile ox-drawn siege towers, and featured bridges over streams and other obstacles.

When the region eventually became part of the Roman Empire in the early years CE, the Romans built roads over the ancient Persian roads, improving some sections of existing road by laying a hard-packed gravelled surface and curbing it with stone blocks. As some of these Roman roads are still used today, this means that parts of the Persian Royal Road have been in continual use for around three millennia.

ALEXANDER THE GREAT

The next significant phase in the Silk Road's development came when Alexander the Great expanded the Greek Empire into Central Asia. Born in around 356BCE, Alexander III of Macedon succeeded his father, Philip II, in 336BCE. Within just 13 years, he conquered the Persian Empire, Egypt, Assyria and northern India, and built one of the largest empires in ancient history, stretching from Greece to the Indus River.

As he made his way across the Middle East and Central Asia, conquering peoples and occupying their land, Alexander founded numerous cities, which he humbly named after himself. According to the Greek biographer Plutarch, he founded at least 70 cities, although many were undoubtedly pre-existing settlements that he renamed and/or repopulated; the number he directly founded is closer to 20. Some of these would go on to become important trading hubs on the Silk Road, notably Alexandria in Egypt and Alexandria Eschate or 'Alexandria the Furthest' (modern Khujand in Tajikistan) at the mouth of the Ferghana Valley.

When the Greek army moved south, across the Khyber Pass into what is now Pakistan, a contingent of soldiers, many of them wounded veterans, remained behind, settling among the Sogdian people, where they watched out for rebellions and helped defend trade routes. Alexander's habit of establishing settlements in conquered territories played a major role in the foundation of the

Silk Road by creating strong links. He was also instrumental in opening up the maritime Silk Road, equipping a fleet to carry some of his troops from the mouth of the Indus River to the head of the Persian Gulf, to determine whether it would be feasible to sail from Mesopotamia to India.

Following Alexander's death at the age of 33 in 323BCE, his empire (divided between four of his generals) began to unravel, but the flowering of trade thanks to its coherence continued. He had helped to create a uniform economic and cultural world that stretched from Europe into Central Asia, and with it a unified trade area; local merchants also benefited from the release of Persian bullion.

Trade continued to grow under one of his successors, the Ptolemaic dynasty, which ruled over Egypt. Through its dominion over the Red Sea ports, the dynasty promoted trade with Mesopotamia,

Alexander the Great (c. 356–323BCE) played an important role in the development of the Silk Road, establishing linked settlements in widespread territories as he conquered them.

India and East Africa, with assistance from intermediaries such as the Nabataeans and other Arabs.

The Greeks remained in Central Asia for about 300 years after Alexander's death. During this Hellenistic age, the ancient world was dominated by a Graeco-Oriental culture. Many of the Macedonian soldiers left behind in Central Asia intermarried with the indigenous populace, and, initially under the Seleucid Empire – Alexander's successor in that part of his territory – the settlements in the east gradually morphed into the Graeco-Bactrian Kingdom in Bactria and Sogdiana, and then the Indo-Greek Kingdom in what is now northern India/Pakistan and eastern Afghanistan. While the culture of these kingdoms was essentially Greek, over the next 200 or so years they became increasingly isolated from the West, and Eastern elements became more dominant.

Easterly expansion continued nonetheless, particularly during the reign of the Graeco-Bactrian king Euthydemus I, who extended control beyond Alexandria Eschate. It's believed that he led expeditions as far as Kashgar in Chinese Turkestan, which brought the first known contact between China and the West in around 200BCE, paving the way for the opening of organized trade between the two and setting the scene for the Silk Road.

Alexandria
Founded in around 331BCE by Alexander the Great, Alexandria grew quickly to become the second-most-powerful city of the ancient world after Rome. For almost 1,000 years, it served as the capital of Hellenistic, Roman and Byzantine Egypt and a centre of Mediterranean trade, a vital hub on the maritime routes between Asia and Europe.

Before the arrival of Alexander and his troops, the site held a city named Rhakotis, whose origins dated back to

1500BCE. Alexander wanted the new city to supersede Naucratis as a Hellenistic centre in Egypt, while also providing a link between Greece and the fertile Nile valley. The site offered several advantages: Pharos island screened the harbour; it was far enough away from the Nile to be spared silt deposition but close enough that a canal could be built to provide fresh water; and the vast Libyan Desert to the west and the Nile Delta to the east offered protection against invading armies. Alexander himself only spent a few months in the nascent city before leaving Egypt, never to return. His viceroy Cleomenes oversaw its continued development.

Alexandria replaced Tyre (recently sacked by Alexander's troops) as a centre of trade on the maritime Silk Road, its safe anchorage making it an attractive transit point for merchants passing between the Mediterranean and the Red Sea. Consequently it grew rapidly; just a century after its foundation, it was the world's largest city.

Following Alexander's death in 323BCE, Alexandria became the capital of the Ptolemaic Kingdom. As a trade centre, and thus a prosperous melting pot of cultural influences, it became the intellectual and cultural centre of the ancient world. Home to the Great Library of Alexandria, it attracted many scholars, including Euclid and Archimedes.

The city was annexed by the Romans in 80BCE. At that time, Egypt was a major grain-producing region and the Romans were largely dependent on Egyptian grain, so Alexandria was strategically important. When the Roman Empire began to collapse, Alexandria's influence declined and during the seventh century, 975 years of Graeco-Roman control ended, with the Persians, Byzantines and Arabs wrestling for dominance.

After it fell to the Arabs in 641, despite access to the trade networks of the early Islamic Caliphate, which was expanding into Central Asia and across northern Africa, a slow decline began. In 1365, the city was brutally sacked by a Crusader army led by King Peter of Cyprus.

The opening of the sea route to India around the Cape of Good Hope during the late 15th century saw the volume of trade passing through Alexandria's port dwindle. Within just a few decades, it fell to the Ottoman Empire and remained under Ottoman rule until 1798, by which time it was little more than a fishing village.

Under an industrialization programme in the 19th century, Alexandria began to return to its former glory, once again becoming a major centre of international maritime trade. Today, it is Egypt's second-largest city, with a population of more than five million people, and the country's leading port.

— 2 —
THE RISE
OF THE
SILK ROAD

By the start of the second century BCE, the stage was set for the opening up of the Silk Road proper. Wealthy elites existed at either end of an existing trade network, in China and Rome, craving luxury products from the opposite end.

CHINA AND THE EASTERN SILK ROAD

In 206BCE, China's Han dynasty was founded by Liu Bang, a minor official who led a successful revolt against the repressive Qin dynasty. He went on to become the Emperor Gaozu, establishing the imperial capital in the city of Chang'an (near modern Xi'an), which sat at the convergence of many of the country's primary roads.

At the time, settlements on China's northern and western borders were suffering regular attacks from the nomadic tribes of the Xiongnu, recently joined together in a confederation. The Qin Emperor had attempted to keep them at bay by connecting a series of walls built by previous states to form what would become the Great Wall of China. This having proved insufficient protection, the Han tried to foster good relations with the Xiongnu by bribing them with large quantities of silk textiles and a silk padding known as floss, which the nomads used to make clothing and bedding that was both warm and lightweight.

Starting in 198BCE, the Han also instituted the *heqin* policy, whereby 'princesses' – typically women from minor branches of the royal family – were married off to rulers of powerful enemy states, including the Xiongnu, as appeasement. They were usually accompanied by a further bribe, in the form of a large dowry of silk and other luxury products. However, the policy was only nominally successful and Xiongnu attacks continued.

In 141 BCE, when Emperor Wudi ascended the throne of the Han dynasty, his first task was dealing with the nomads in the north. He sent a series of military expeditions to the steppe that not only

A painting from the Song dynasty (1127–1279) illustrates the heartbreaking story of Cai Wenji, a woman from the Han dynasty period who was abducted by the Xiongnu.

succeeded in pushing back the harassers but also captured large herds of sheep and horses.

Wudi learnt that one of China's traditional allies, the Yuezhi, were also in conflict with the Xiongnu, and decided to see if they would be interested in forming an alliance against their common enemy. However, the route west to Yuezhi territory passed through land controlled by the Xiongnu; the only member of the Han court willing to make the journey was a petty official by the name of Zhang Qian.

In 139BCE, Zhang Qian and a party of 100 set out. But when they reached the Hexi (or Gansu) Corridor – a strip of land in modern Gansu province bordered by the Yellow River to the east (Hexi means 'west of the river'), the Mongolian deserts to the north and the Qilian Mountains to the south – they were promptly captured and imprisoned by the Xiongnu. Zhang Qian spent the next decade in captivity, moving with the Xiongnu imperial camp as it travelled around the steppe. He married a Xiongnu woman and fathered several children with her.

Then, in 129BCE, he escaped and made his way to the territory of Dayuan (modern Ferghana in Tajikistan/Uzbekistan/Kyrgyzstan; Dayuan's capital was Alexandria Eschate), whose king escorted him southwest to Sogdiana. From there, he was able to reach the court of the Yuezhi, which was then located on the banks of the Oxus River in Bactria (the Amu Darya in modern Afghanistan). In around 176BCE, the Yuezhi had suffered a humiliating defeat at the hands of the Xiongnu and been forced out of their homeland in what is now China's Gansu province. Migrating west, they ended up in Bactria.

On reaching the Yuezhi court, Zhang Qian entreated them to join the Han against the Xiongnu, but in vain. He spent a year with the Yuezhi before setting out for Chang'an, but was again captured by the Xiongnu. This time his captivity lasted only a year, as turmoil in the camp allowed him to escape with his wife and children.

When Zhang Qian finally returned to the Han court, 13 years

Zhang Qian's missions across the steppe introduced the Chinese to new products hitherto unknown to them. He is revered as a national hero for his role in opening China to the world of commercial trade.

— TIMELINE —

209BCE	*Xiongnu confederation forms*
206BCE	*Start of Western Han dynasty*
139BCE	*Emperor Wu dispatches Zhang Qian on fact-finding mission to Central Asia*
130BCE	*Start of Kushan Empire*
126BCE	*Zhang Qian returns to China*
121BCE	*Chinese take control of the Hexi Corridor*
102BCE	*General Li Guangli dispatched to bring back horses from the Dawan*
63BCE	*End of Seleucid Empire*
53BCE	*Romans see silk for the first time at the battle of Carrhae*
30BCE	*Roman conquest of Egypt*
27BCE	*Start of the Roman Empire*
9CE	*Start of Xin dynasty*
24CE	*Start of Eastern Han dynasty*
97CE	*Gan Ying attempts to reach Rome*
220	*Start of Three Kingdoms period in China*
227	*Sassanids replace the Parthians in Mesopotamia*
266	*Start of Jin dynasty*
375	*End of the Kushan Empire*
420	*Start of Northern and Southern dynasties*
476	*Fall of the Western Roman Empire*

after he had left, he relayed his experiences in the 'Western Regions' to the emperor. Of particular interest to Wudi were two elements: trade and horses. During visits to markets in Bactria, Zhang Qian was impressed by the exotic goods for sale, including glassware and large, powerful horses.

He spoke to traders about a particular type of bamboo and cloth they were selling. Zhang Qian knew that they had been produced in the Shu region of southwest China but he was told that the goods came from India, a region unknown to China. The news that there was international trade in Chinese goods was tantalizing, but had to be tempered with the fact that the only known overland trade routes travelled across the steppe and were thus under control of the Xiongnu. Zhang Qian suggested that the movement of goods from the Shu region to India implied the existence of a more direct route, but when Wudi sent an expedition along the only possible land route, through mountainous Yunnan (in modern southwest China), it was attacked by the inhabitants, who were clearly nervous about Chinese expansion.

And then there were the horses. Zhang Qian's tales of the mighty steeds of Dayuan – known as 'blood-sweating horses' and believed to be the progeny born from interbreeding of mortal and heavenly horses – were of particular interest to Wudi. The emperor knew that such horses, larger and faster than China's, would come in very handy in his war against the Xiongnu.

As the Han continued their campaign against the Xiongnu, they managed to push them back to the point where they were no longer a direct threat to farming settlements along China's northern border. This allowed Wudi to focus on wresting control of the trade routes to the Western Regions. He sent one of his generals, Wei Qing, with a large cavalry force to attack the Xiongnu, and over the next few years the Han general won a series of decisive battles. He was later joined by his nephew, Huo Qubing, who continued the successful campaign, and by 121BCE the Chinese were in control of the Hexi Corridor. The emperor ordered his generals to crush the

Xiongnu for good, and they routed the nomads, forcing them deep into the steppe.

The Xiongnu

From the third century BCE to the end of the first century CE, the nomadic Xiongnu peoples were the dominant power on the eastern Asian steppe, centred in what is now Mongolia.

Chinese expansion into Xiongnu territory during the Qin dynasty is thought to have been the trigger that led to the tribes uniting into a confederacy in 209 BCE. From then on, they were a constant thorn in China's side, making regular raids on its northern and western settlements. After a series of heavy military defeats, the Chinese attempted to halt these border raids by extending the Great Wall, sending princesses to marry Xiongnu leaders and bribing them with valuable gifts. But when the Xiongnu repeatedly broke the peace treaties, the Chinese resorted to all-out war. However, being nomadic, the Xiongnu were able to simply disperse in the face of defeat, before banding together again for another attack. Nevertheless, the Han Chinese eventually pushed them back far enough to control the territory through which the nascent Silk Road passed, although Xiongnu bandits continued to harass travellers.

During the first century BCE, a series of internal struggles split the confederacy into two factions, one of which sided with the Chinese. From then on, Xiongnu power began to wane, and during the first half of the fifth century the last remaining vestiges of the Xiongnu were effectively assimilated into China.

By this time, Wudi had begun to extend the Great Wall to the west and now he ordered construction to begin in the Hexi

Corridor in order to protect the new trade route. The corridor is a broad strip of relatively flat arid grassland, punctuated by a series of oases formed by meltwater from the mountains; although agriculture was feasible, it was extremely labour-intensive as the surrounding sand dunes were constantly encroaching on the crops and irrigation channels. The Han government's solution was to kill two birds with one stone by sending soldiers and their families to both protect the trade routes and develop the region's agricultural potential. They were joined by thousands of settlers, both volunteer and conscripted.

The Great Wall was eventually extended all the way to the town of Dunhuang, which became an important garrison, housing large numbers of Chinese troops. About 80 km (50 miles) northwest of the town was the Yumen Pass, otherwise known as the Jade Gate, the westernmost passage through the Great Wall and thus the first entry into China for travellers heading east and the final frontier

The Yumen Pass or Jade Gate, erected in c. 121 BCE, was a frontier post to the west of Dunhuang. It was named for the quantities of jade that were transported through it.

for those heading west. Named for the numerous jade-carrying caravans that passed through on their way to China from the oasis town of Khotan (modern Hotan in China's Xinjiang province), the Jade Gate served as both a guard post and a customs station, where caravans passing to and from China were forced to pay taxes based on the value of the goods they were carrying.

The Great Wall of China

The Great Wall is the world's longest manmade structure. Construction began during the seventh century BCE under the Chu state, which built a stretch of continuous wall from today's Hubei to Henan to defend China's central plain against the kingdoms of the north. By the time construction ceased at the end of the Ming dynasty in 1644, the wall stretched more than 21,000 km (13,000 miles) and crossed 15 Chinese regions, from what is now Liaoning on the coast to Xinjiang in the east. At its highest point, it is 8 m (26 ft) tall; at its broadest, 9.1 m (30 ft) wide at the base and 3.7 m (12 ft) at the top.

During the period when the Silk Road was first opening up, around 140BCE, China's northern provinces suffered regular attacks from the Xiongnu, putting trade under threat. In response, the Han court extended the Great Wall and strengthened existing sections.

As there were only a limited number of gates through the wall, these became centres of trade. Inns, restaurants and tea stalls sprang up to support travellers, whose wares were sold in outdoor markets, booths and shops that lined the narrow streets on either side of the wall. Gates also served as border-control points, where immigration and emigration could be controlled and duties on trade goods collected. The wall itself also served as a transportation corridor.

The Great Wall was constructed as a defence against attack and for border control, facilitating the imposition of duties on goods transported along the Silk Road. Its imposing bulk is made of stone, brick, tamped earth, wood and other materials.

The next significant period of construction took place during the Ming dynasty. The new sections were stronger and more elaborate, using bricks and stone blocks. It's thought that as many as 25,000 watchtowers were built along the wall at this time.

The Cultural Revolution (1966–76) saw large stretches of the wall destroyed, with stone blocks removed for use in construction elsewhere. Then, during the 1980s, as China began to open up to the West, restoration and preservation became a focus for the reformist leader Deng Xiaoping, who initiated a 'Love our China and restore our Great Wall' campaign. In 1987, it was placed on the World Heritage list. Today, less than ten per cent of the Ming wall remains intact, but the restored sections draw tourists from around the globe, with more than ten million visitors each year.

Dunhuang was strategically important because of its position at the western end of the Hexi Corridor, but also because it was the point where the three main Silk Road trade routes converged. These allowed travellers to navigate through and around the Tarim Basin, a vast arid bowl encircled by some of the world's highest mountains and containing the treacherous Taklamakan Desert, a waterless sand sea that covers an area larger than modern France. The northern route led across the 'White Dragon Desert', a journey of about 650 km (400 miles) to the oasis towns of Hami and Turfan; the central route followed the northern fringes of the Lop Nor salt marsh (now desert), heading 500 km (300 miles) due west to another oasis outpost, Loulan; and the southern route was an 800-km (500-mile) track to the oasis settlement of Cherchen. Going further west, the three routes became two, a northern and southern route that converged on the city of Kashgar at the foot of the Pamir Mountains.

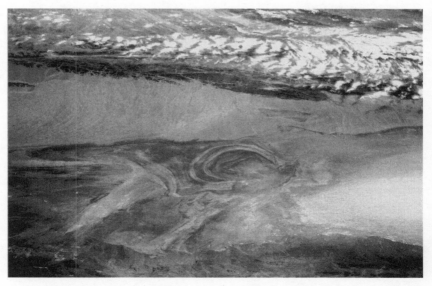

A satellite image of the Lop Nur basin in the Desert of Lop (formerly the Sea of Lop Nur) in modern-day Xinjiang, China. The Wusun people originally lived near here before the area was taken over by the Xiongnu in the second century BCE.

More than 30 oasis kingdoms controlled territory – including sections of the different trade routes – around the outer fringe of the Tarim Basin. They offered sanctuaries for caravans to rest, recuperate and resupply, but they could also block further progress or demand payment. Many of them were subject to extortion by the Xiongnu, forced to pay tribute in the form of food and valuable commodities such as jade and silk.

Wudi realized that alliances with these kingdoms would have multiple benefits: by removing a source of supplies and wealth, they would weaken the Xiongnu; they could be used to bolster Chinese forces in the region; and they would help keep the trade routes open. He sent envoys to establish contact with their rulers, offering bales of the finest silk and other valuable goods in return for support against the Xiongnu. A few rulers signed up, but most opted to wait and see how events unfolded.

Dunhuang

Dunhuang was one of the most important cities of the early Silk Road, a crossroads for the three branches that ran around the Tarim Basin. Situated at an oasis on the edge of the Taklamakan Desert, it was one of the first trading cities encountered by travellers arriving in China from the west. It also controlled the entrance to the Hexi Corridor, which led to the ancient Chinese capitals of Chang'an and Luoyang.

The area around Dunhuang was first settled in around 2000BCE and was variously controlled by the Yuezhi and Xiongnu. When the latter were driven out by the Han Chinese in around 121BCE, Dunhuang became a Chinese garrison town, protecting the region and its trade routes. Around this time, the Great Wall was extended to Dunhuang, a clear signal of its importance to Silk Road trade. By the early years CE, the town had a population of almost 40,000 and was a vital supply point for passing traders.

> *Dunhuang means 'blazing beacon', a reference to the signal fires that were lit to communicate news of enemy movements to outposts to the east in the Hexi Corridor.*

Early in its history, Dunhuang became a centre for Buddhism, and during the fourth century local monks started to carve caves into the friable rock nearby as sites for meditation. A century later, they began painting scenes from Buddha's life in the caves, which eventually became places of worship and pilgrimage. The Mogao Caves, or Caves of the Thousand Buddhas, eventually numbered almost 500.

This silk scroll found in the Mogao Caves dates from 968 and is entitled Guanyin of the Water Moon. *Guanyin is a Buddhist bodhisattva associated with compassion and mercy.*

When China's regional power began to wane at the end of the Tang dynasty in the early tenth century, Dunhuang was engulfed in turmoil once more. It enjoyed a period of semi-independence, but was also conquered at various times by the Chinese, Tibetans, Uighurs and Mongols, who sacked the town in 1227 and then rebuilt it. When trade on the Silk Road waned during the 14th century, Dunhuang's fortunes similarly declined. China regained control in around 1715.

The city re-entered popular consciousness at the start of the 20th century, when it began to be visited by European explorers and archaeologists. In 1907, the British-Hungarian archaeologist Sir Marc Aurel Stein recovered an extraordinary cache of scrolls from a small walled-up room in one of the Mogao Caves. Dunhuang's cosmopolitan nature is reflected in the diversity of languages in which the texts were written: Chinese, Tibetan, Sanskrit, Khotanese, Uighur and Sogdian, as well as a Hebrew prayer that was probably carried as a talisman. Today, Dunhuang has a population of around 200,000.

In 119BCE, Wudi sent Zhang Qian on a new mission as an envoy to the Wusun, a nomadic society based just to the west of the Xiongnu territory, in the hope of forming an alliance. The emperor provided Zhang Qian with 300 followers, tens of thousands of cattle and sheep, and 600 horses carrying a fortune in gold and silk. Although the mission didn't achieve its primary objective, by sending deputy envoys to other surrounding states Zhang Qian helped to expand China's trade network. News of China's military success against the Xiongnu was spreading across the Western Regions and the Silk Road was soon busy with envoys making their way to the Chinese capital to pay tribute. However, given the great distances involved, the Han government found it difficult to control its frontier territory and was repeatedly forced to send armies to subdue restless states and keep the remaining Xiongnu in check.

Shortly afterwards, in 102BCE, Wudi dispatched envoys bearing gold and silk to the king of Dayuan in the hope of buying some of his fabled horses. But not only was the king disinclined to sell any of his steeds, he killed the envoy. Not so easily deterred, Wudi sent an army to Dayuan to take the horses by force. It was initially rebuffed, having run out of supplies during the journey across the Taklamakan Desert. When it returned to the Great Wall, however, Wudi threatened to have any soldier attempting to enter the Jade Gate killed. He resupplied the forces and provided significant reinforcements, and the army returned to Dayuan. After a 40-day siege of the capital, Alexandria Eschate, the Chinese managed to breach an outer wall and cut off the city's water supply. The nobles killed the king and offered to provide the Chinese with as many horses as they desired. The army headed back to China with 3,000 heavenly horses; however, only a third made it back to the Jade Gate. This military success was enough to persuade many more of the Tarim kingdoms to ally themselves with the Chinese, who established military garrisons in several oasis settlements.

Wudi's death in 87BCE finally shattered the fragile peace in the Western Regions. Only in 60BCE did Emperor Xuan establish the Protectorate of the Western Regions in Wulei (modern Luntai, on the northern edge of the Tarim Basin) to supervise the 36 states that sprawled across the vast area, and once again the Silk Road became busy.

There followed a period of turmoil within China itself, as Wang Mang usurped the throne and established the Xin dynasty. The Tarim kingdoms refused to accept his authority and China lost control of the Western Regions. Even after Emperor Guangwu re-established the Han dynasty in 25CE, with its new capital in Luoyang, the focus remained on rebuilding Chinese society, at the expense of the Western Regions and the security of the Silk Road.

Emperor Guangwu (5BCE–57CE), depicted here by the Tang artist Yan Liben (600–673), had little interest in external affairs and focused his attention on the new capital at Luoyang.

By this time, the Xiongnu had split into two rival factions: the Southern Xiongnu, allied with China, and the Northern Xiongnu, which continued to oppose the Chinese. From its base in the Tarim

Basin, the Northern Xiongnu invaded the Hexi Corridor, once again disrupting Silk Road trade.

As relative stability returned to China, the Han court's attention turned again to the Western Regions. In 73CE, the emperor sent a general named Ban Chao to the Tarim Basin to pacify it. Although he only led a small contingent of soldiers, he was able to play on dissension among the tribes to divide and conquer. He was sent back there again four years later, then made *duhu* (protector general) of the Western Regions in 91CE and controlled the area for a further 11 years, quashing rebellions, repelling invaders and establishing diplomatic relations with more than 50 of the surrounding states.

When the ageing Ban Chao returned to Luoyang in 102CE, the peace in the Western Regions began to unravel. In 107CE, many of the protectorate's dependent states rebelled, once again threatening the safety of the Silk Road, and the Chinese were forced out of the Western Regions for more than a decade.

In 123CE, the emperor sent Ban Chao's youngest son, Ban Yong, with 500 ex-convict soldiers to again pacify the region. Like his father, Ban Yong was a capable commander and, through a series of strategic alliances and military successes, he consolidated Han control over the Western Regions.

Towards the end of the second century, China entered another period of internal turmoil, as a series of peasant rebellions and power struggles among the elites saw the country divide into three warring kingdoms. A procession of dynasties followed, many short-lived, and northern China broke up into a collection of independent kingdoms, mostly ruled by non-Chinese. Amid widespread warfare, many Chinese migrated south and by the early fifth century, China was being ruled by parallel regimes in the north and south.

ROME AND THE WESTERN SILK ROAD

In 141BCE, having already taken Bactria and Media, the new leader of Parthia (modern northeast Iran), Mithridates I, captured the Seleucid capital and had himself crowned king. A large part of the Silk Road's route now came under Parthian rule, giving the Parthians control of trade in the region, hence they became the main intermediaries between China and the West – where the rise of Rome fuelled a growing appetite for trade and luxury goods.

Meanwhile, knowing about the Parthians from Zhang Qian, in 121BCE the Han court sent a diplomatic delegation to the court of Mithridates II, who had succeeded Mithridates I. The Chinese hoped that the Parthians would join them against the Xiongnu, but their offer of an alliance was rebuffed. They did, however, open trade relations with Parthia. Such relations were of great value to the Parthians, who taxed the silk-carrying caravans that travelled west along the Silk Road. They also carried on their own trade in spices, perfume and fruit with the Chinese and in iron, spices and leather with the Romans. Traders making their way east to China brought a mixture of western Asian and Roman goods, including luxury glassware.

A Parthian relief of Mithridates I of Parthia at Xong-e Ashdar – now the city of Izeh, Khouzestan province, Iran.

Maes Titianus

Born into a family of Macedonian merchants, Maes Titianus was a Roman citizen and a merchant himself. It's believed that he lived in the city of Tyre in what is now Lebanon, but there is much debate about when he lived, with competing theories positing either the start or the end of the first century CE. Either way, Maes Titianus organized an expedition to China aimed at gaining a commercial advantage over his rivals – in particular, direct access to Chinese silk.

The expedition travelled through the territory of the Parthian and Kushan kingdoms before being intercepted by Chinese forces near the Pamirs. The travellers were transported to the capital and presented to the Han court.

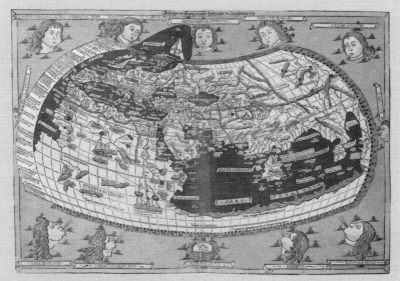

Claudius Ptolemy's 15th-century depiction of the Ecumene ('the known world'). In drawing the map, Ptolemy used information gained by the expedition to China organized by Maes Titianus.

Because they spoke Greek and had been travelling as part of a Parthian caravan, the Chinese were unaware that they were Roman subjects. The merchants presented the emperor with rewoven Syrian silks and imperial gold coins and received Han silks as diplomatic gifts.

When the expedition returned, two years after it had departed, the knowledge it had gained spread across the Roman world. The Graeco-Roman geographer Claudius Ptolemy used details of the journey to draw new maps of Asia, more accurately locating China.

During the first century BCE, as the Parthians continued to expand their empire across Mesopotamia, the Roman Empire was doing the same, conquering both the remnants of the Seleucid Empire and the Ptolemaic Empire based in Egypt. Trade along the Silk Road blossomed. The Romans took over the existing eastern Silk Road trade routes, which connected Asia, the Hellenistic powers and the Arabs. Control of these brought new luxuries to the elites of the Roman Empire and enriched the empire as a whole.

The Romans were uncomfortable with the powerful presence of the Parthians on their eastern border, and trade along the Silk Road was regularly interrupted by intermittent wars between the two powers. One such battle had particular significance for Silk Road trade. In 53 BCE, a Roman commander, Crassus, led a large army across the Euphrates frontier and into Parthia. He was met by a significantly smaller force of Parthian cavalry. As the Parthian forces began their charge at the Roman infantry, they unfurled a series of colourful banners made from a strange, light fabric unlike anything the Romans had seen before: silk. The Romans were defeated, their commander killed, but some soldiers survived and news of the ethereal cloth spread to their homeland.

East meets West

Remarkably, the first direct contact between Rome and China didn't occur until 166CE (after the Roman Empire had defeated the Parthians and taken control of the Persian Gulf), when a Roman delegation reached the Han court via the Maritime Silk Road. Thought to have been sent by Emperor Marcus Aurelius, the envoys arrived in China after a journey of more than 14 months.

When they were brought before the Chinese emperor in Luoyang, the delegation confirmed the existence of an overland route between China and the Roman Empire, and explained that Rome had been attempting for some time to make contact with the Chinese, but that efforts had been blocked by the Parthians. The Chinese had already heard tales of the distant, powerful and, most importantly, rich empire to the west, but were disappointed by the gifts that the envoys had brought. In trade negotiations such as these, it was customary for envoys to shower their hosts with valuable merchandise, but all the Romans had to offer were some elephant tusks, rhinoceros horn and turtle shell.

It's possible that they had been forced to sell their more valuable goods to finance their journey, but regardless, the Chinese were less than impressed with their offerings. It seems likely that the emperor concluded that the Roman Empire was neither as wealthy nor as ambitious as he had been led to believe. There is no record of the delegation successfully returning to Rome, so the contact probably had little lasting impact on Silk Road trade.

Traders were often forced to take alternative routes to avoid conflicts, particularly in the region around the Euphrates River. While the wars were about control of territory, the underlying motive was increasingly control of trade, attendant profits and access to luxury goods. Hence, despite the regular conflict, trade and communication among the powers along the Silk Road were becoming increasingly regular and organized.

During the first to the third centuries, Central Asia and northern India were united by the Kushan Empire. Descended from the Yuezhi nomads who had been forced from the steppe by the Xiongnu, the Kushans began to expand their territory in around 50CE, crossing the Hindu Kush and moving into northern India. They came to control both the steppe and oasis routes of the overland Silk Road through Central Asia and on into western India, as well as, eventually, a number of ports vital to Silk Road trade, particularly with Rome. Additionally, in 106CE, the Romans took control of the Nabataean city of Petra, which was part of the vital trading network through the desert. This control generated vast wealth for the empire.

The Kushan Empire was also a source of goods that were in demand at either end of the Silk Road, including plant-based dyes and medicines, incense and precious stones such as lapis lazuli and turquoise. These minerals, mined in what is now Afghanistan and Iran respectively, were carried to the prosperous Indian Ocean port of Barbarikon, at the mouth of the Indus River (near modern-day Karachi in Pakistan). The port was important for materials from outside the empire too, including furs from China and Central Asia, silk yarn from China and cotton cloth and indigo dye from India.

Petra
With its dramatic monuments carved into sheer sandstone cliffs, the ancient city of Petra is one of the most impressive archaeological sites in the Middle East. At the height of its splendour in the first century CE, it was a central player in the spice and incense trade.

Known as the 'rose city' due to the colour of its sandstone, Petra ('rock' in Greek) lies in what is now southwest Jordan, on a strategically important route through the mountains on the eastern flank of the Arabah Valley south of the Dead Sea. It's believed that it was established during the fourth century BCE as the capital of the Nabataean Kingdom.

The Nabataeans were nomadic Bedouin livestock herders. Living in a region with low, unpredictable rainfall and little in the way of natural water sources, they became highly skilled at utilizing and controlling water, harvesting and storing both rainwater and floodwater. This allowed them to adopt a more settled lifestyle and succeed as traders, controlling the routes that brought incense (frankincense and myrrh) from southern Arabia to cities on the Mediterranean coast and brought spices and textiles in the other direction. They used the wealth accumulated to build Petra, which they turned into a major regional trading hub.

While the city's position within a towering canyon meant fortress-like protection, its success resulted from its impressive water conduit system. Flash floods are frequent in the area, and the Nabataeans used dams, cisterns and pipes to both control the floods and store the precious water they brought, which was supplemented by water from a perennial spring. So effective were their works that the city could sometimes sell surplus water to passing caravans. The Nabataeans had, in effect, created an artificial oasis.

They were also skilled stone carvers. They cut hundreds of elaborate tombs into the cliffs, along with a Roman-style theatre that could seat 3,000 people and numerous obelisks, temples, sacrificial altars and colonnaded streets. Caravans entering the city from the east were forced to pass through

El Deir ('The Monastery') is Petra's largest monument and dates from the first century BCE. As the capital city of the Nabataean Kingdom, it was a centre of trade and provided both strong rock-cut protection and an advanced water-conduit system.

the Siq ('the shaft'), a dark, narrow gorge only 3–4 m (10–13 ft) wide in places, before being confronted by the impressive façade of Al Khazneh ('the treasury').

Petra's population is thought to have peaked at about 20,000 before, in 106CE, it fell to the Romans. Although it continued to flourish for a while, soon the rise of the Silk Road, both overland through Parthia and via the maritime routes, and of Palmyra, saw its fortunes decline. Earthquakes damaged the city – and its vital water-management system – in 363 and 551. By 700 it was empty.

The ruins served as a Crusader outpost during the 12th century, but the city was only rediscovered by the West in 1812 by the Swiss explorer Johann Ludwig Burckhardt. It was added to the World Heritage list in 1985 and is now a popular tourist destination, receiving about 600,000 visitors in 2017.

In 227, control of southern Mesopotamia passed from the Parthians to the Sassanid dynasty, based in what is now southern Iran. The arrival of the Sassanids blocked Rome's access to the Persian Gulf via the prosperous oasis city of Palmyra. They also took on the Kushan Empire, annexing its northern territory and thus closing off access to the steppe. The Palmyrenes fought back, repelling an attempted Sassanid invasion in 267 and then expanding their territory at the expense of the Roman Empire. Unsurprisingly, this episode didn't end well for Palmyra, with the city razed by the Roman Emperor Aurelian in 275 after a rebellion against Rome.

Despite the turmoil in the region, trade continued to flow along the Silk Road. Oasis towns expanded, aided by improvements in irrigation and well-building technology. However, by the beginning of the fourth century, cracks were beginning to form in Rome's empire. Barbarians were attacking its western frontiers and there was increasing unrest among the peoples it had subjugated. Weakened by unsuccessful military campaigns against the Sassanids, riven by civil war and unable to fight back effectively against barbarian attacks or uprisings in its far-flung territories, the Western Roman Empire finally collapsed in around 476 (although the Eastern Roman, or Byzantine, Empire would survive for a further thousand years).

The end of the empire had a significant effect on Silk Road trade as the European demand for luxury products from the east largely ended too. But this proved merely a readjustment, and trade continued to flow along the routes.

Palmyra

Built in an oasis about halfway between the Mediterranean and the Euphrates River in what is now Syria, Palmyra was the most important trading hub in the Middle East, connecting Rome, Mesopotamia and the East, and became one of the ancient world's prime cultural centres. Originally known as Tadmor, it was named Palmyra ('city of palm trees') by the Romans during the first century CE.

The first recorded mention of Palmrya dates back to about 2000BCE, but it only rose to prominence in the third century BCE, when it became a key staging post for travelling merchants. Effectively the easternmost entrance to Roman markets, it grew wealthy off the caravan trade; its citizens traded with both Romans and Parthians, and established outposts along the Silk Road and throughout the Parthian and Roman empires.

Independent for most of its early history, the city came under Roman control during the reign of Emperor Tiberius in around 14CE. But, benefiting from privileged status within the empire – it retained much internal autonomy – it enjoyed great prosperity, especially when control over the Arabian Peninsula's southern trade routes was effectively handed to the Palmyrenes after Petra fell to the Romans in 106CE.

In recognition of its importance to trade, Palmyra was declared a *civitas libera* ('free city') by Emperor Hadrian after he visited in around 129CE. Many of its most important architectural features, including the theatre, sections of the grand colonnaded street that forms the axis of the city and the Temple of Nabu, date from this period.

During the third century, regional instability affected trade, especially after the Sassanids replaced the Parthians in Persia and southern Mesopotamia. The new rulers disbanded Palmyrene colonies in their territory, closed the road to the Persian Gulf to Palmyrene trade and declared war against the Romans. In response, the Palmyrenes began a military build-up of their own and even began to expand their territory, conquering Roman Arabia, Egypt and most of Anatolia in 270. These successes led Palmyra to declare independence from Rome, but two years later the Roman emperor Aurelian regained Anatolia and then razed Palmyra. Although the city was later rebuilt, its size was greatly reduced.

In 634, Palmyra was conquered by the Rashidun Caliphate. This began a period of rule by a series of Arab caliphates and decline as a trading centre. Earthquakes devastated the city in 1068 and 1089. During the 13th and 14th centuries it was controlled by the Mamluks, then destroyed by the Timurids in 1400. The remnants became part of the Ottoman Empire in 1516.

During the 17th and 18th centuries, the ruined city was rediscovered by travellers; after Syria became part of the French Mandate in the 1920s, archaeological excavations began under the general director of antiquities in Syria, Henri Arnold Seyrig.

Palmyra's ruins were added to the World Heritage list in 1980. In 2015, the extremist group known as Islamic State in Iraq and the Levant took control of the site and set about destroying several of its most important monuments, including the Temple of Baal Shamen and Palmyra's main temple, the Temple of Bel.

— 3 —
THE GOLDEN AGE
OF THE
SILK ROAD

The Silk Road always functioned best during periods of relative political stability, which is one reason why it entered its golden age during the Tang dynasty in the seventh century. Under the Tang, China became the world's most powerful and prosperous nation. That prosperity was another factor in the Silk Road's success, as was China's friendlier diplomatic policy and the relative stability at the western end of the Silk Road – the Byzantine Empire, along with the Sassanids in Persia and then the Arabian Empire – which helped to keep trade prosperous and provided markets for Chinese goods. Chang'an and other Chinese urban centres became increasingly cosmopolitan as merchants, travellers and envoys from all over Eurasia were welcomed into a more open China. Increasingly, foreigners came to live and trade there, drawn by the profits to be made.

TANG DYNASTY

The first Tang emperor, Gaozu, managed to unite most of China and rejuvenate the Chinese economy, keeping his administration small, distributing land to every taxable male, creating mints and establishing a new copper coinage. During the 630s, his successor, Taizong, launched a number of successful military campaigns in the Western Regions, conquering the oasis states of the Tarim Basin and the Eastern Turkic Khaganate (based in today's Mongolia), among others, and reopening the Silk Road. Although it stayed open for almost 40 years, an incursion by the newly-expansionist Tibetan Empire in 678 effectively closed off the eastern end once more. The next 60 years saw control pass back and forth between the Chinese and Tibetans several times.

With trade booming, the Tang government was unable to produce enough bronze coins to keep up with demand, so it recognized bolts of silk as another form of currency. Payments sent to soldiers manning garrisons in the Western Regions were typically made in silk, which helped to increase trade and sustain the economies of the settlements there. In the first half of the eighth century, China's central government was sending about 900,000 bolts of silk a year to its military headquarters in Hami, Turfan, Beiting and Kucha.

During this golden age, the Silk Road was extended, with new routes forged into Mongolia via the Altai Mountains, and across the Tibetan Plateau and Karakoram range. The northern route around the Taklamakan became increasingly popular, and new towns and markets opened up along it. The trade item most desired by the Tang was horses for its armies; these it bought mainly from nomads from the north, often via Sogdian middlemen.

Notwithstanding such local deals, China's main trading partner was no longer Rome but the Persian world. At first, this meant the Sassanid Empire, successors to the Parthians, who by around 620 controlled the Middle East, the Caucasus, Egypt, large parts of Turkey and much of Central Asia. Sassanid coins served as an international currency all along the Silk Road and the gilded silverware produced by Sassanid craftsmen was widely traded.

In 651, however, the Sassanid Empire was conquered by the Muslim armies of the Rashidun Caliphate, the first of four major caliphates established after the death of Muhammad. Arab expansion continued over the ensuing decades, reaching Central Asia under the Umayyad Caliphate during the eighth century. This period represents the beginning of the Islamic Golden Age, characterized by economic prosperity and a flowering of culture and science.

Trade flourished, and Baghdad, capital of the Abbasid dynasty, rose quickly to become the most important city along the Silk Road.

Emperor Taizong, the second ruler of the Tang dynasty, extended Chinese control of Silk Road territory. This image was created in 641 as part of a scroll painting by the Chinese figure painter Yan Liben.

— TIMELINE —

570	*China's silk monopoly ends*
589	*Sui dynasty unifies China*
618	*Start of Tang dynasty*
651	*Fall of the Sassanian Empire to Arab caliphate armies*
661	*Umayyad Caliphate establishes the first Islamic empire*
704	*Arab armies begin conquest of Central Asia*
750	*Start of the Abbasid Caliphate*
751	*Islamic and Tang armies battle at Talas*
755	*Rebellion in China led by An Lushan*
917	*End of the Tang dynasty*
960	*Start of the Song dynasty*
1037	*Start of the Seljuk Empire*
1127	*Jurchen invade northern China; start of Southern Song dynasty*
1194	*End of the Seljuk Empire*
1206	*Genghis Khan proclaimed ruler of the Mongols*
1271	*Start of the Yuan dynasty; Marco Polo begins his journey*
1299	*Start of Ottoman Empire*
1325	*Ibn Battuta begins his journey*
1330s	*Famines and floods devastate China*
1347	*Black Death reaches Europe*
1368	*Start of the Ming dynasty*

Baghdad

Baghdad began as a Persian village on the banks of the Tigris River, chosen in 762 by al-Mansur, the second caliph of the Abbasid dynasty, for his capital. Thanks to its location at the convergence of several overland and river trade routes, it quickly grew into an important mercantile centre and by the beginning of the ninth century was the world's richest city.

Its riches were also intellectual. The fifth Abbasid caliph, Harun al-Rashid, founded the Khizanat al-Hikma ('Library of Wisdom') which, under his son and successor, al-Ma'mun, became the Baytul-Hikmah or 'House of Wisdom', an unrivalled centre dedicated to research, education and the translation of ancient texts into Arabic. By the middle of the ninth century, it housed the largest book collection in the world. This expansion was spurred on by the establishment of the world's first paper mills in Baghdad towards the end of the eighth century. Mass availability of paper enabled vast amounts of translations and original research to be committed to paper, and libraries and bookstores became increasingly common in the city.

Estimates suggest that Baghdad was home to more than a million inhabitants at its peak during the tenth century, at which point it was probably the world's largest city. By then, however, the Abbasid dynasty was in decline. Subsequent invasion and rule by the Iranian Buwayhids and Seljuk Turks through the tenth and 11th centuries left parts of Baghdad in ruins. It was sacked again in 1258 by Hülegü, a grandson of Genghis Khan, and by Timur in 1401, then ruled by successive Turkmen dynasties. From 1534, it became part of the Ottoman Empire, until its capture by the British during World War I. Under the Ottomans, Baghdad had sunk to the level of a decaying provincial town, home to fewer than 50,000 people.

In modern times, Baghdad has been the capital of the state of Iraq. During the 1970s, relative political stability and oil revenues funded expansion and development, but war with Iran during the 1980s and the Gulf War of 1990–91 saw much of this destroyed. The Iraq War of 2003 brought US troops, and eventually sectarian violence. Today, the city is the second-largest in the Arab world (after Cairo) with a population of almost nine million.

A 15th-century artwork depicts Hülegü Khan's siege of Baghdad in 1258.

China's westward expansion reached its limit in 751 at the Battle of Talas as it vied for control of the Syr Darya region. The area between the Syr Darya (Jaxartes) and Amu Darya (Oxus) rivers (in today's Uzbekistan, Tajikistan, Kyrgyzstan and Kazakhstan), based on Samarkand and Bukhara and incorporating Sogdiana, was known to the West as Transoxiana, the land beyond the

Oxus. Forces from the Abbasid dynasty – which had only the year before overthrown the Umayyads – and their ally, the Tibetan Empire, defeated an army made up of Chinese soldiers and Karluk mercenaries after the mercenaries switched sides mid-battle. As a result, Transoxiana fell under Muslim control and would remain so for the next 400 years. It's believed that China also lost control of the manufacture of paper as a result of the battle, when Chinese soldiers with knowledge of the technology were captured by the Muslim army.

Any hopes that the Tang had of wresting control of Transoxiana from the Abbasids were extinguished in 755 when a rebellion broke out in China after a general named An Lushan declared himself the emperor of northern China. The government withdrew its troops from the Western Regions in order to deal with the rebels. Tax receipts plummeted and the Tang Emperor was forced to hire Uighur mercenaries (a Turkic people from today's Xinjiang).

The An Lushan Rebellion was finally quashed in 763, but by then it had significantly weakened the Tang dynasty, which subsequently lost control of the Western Regions to the Tibetan Empire during the 780s. In 787, Tibetan forces captured Dunhuang and Kucha. They now ruled the southern Tarim Basin and thus controlled the Silk Road. The rebellion represented a turning point for both the Tang dynasty and the Silk Road, which both switched from prosperity to decline. With the withdrawal of Chinese troops – and the injections of government cash they brought – the local economies of the settlements around the Tarim Basin reverted to a subsistence basis.

However, by the 840s, the Tibetan Empire was engulfed in civil war and on the brink of collapse. In 848, a Han Chinese resident of the area around Dunhuang named Zhang Yichao led a local uprising that forced the Tibetans out. He followed this with successful attacks on ten other nearby prefectures with Tibetan garrisons. Once again, the Chinese controlled the Hexi Corridor and Dunhuang, and Silk Road trade could flow again.

Section of a mural from Dunhuang depicting the victory of General Zhang Yichao over the Tibetans in 848.

Meanwhile, the Persian Samanid Empire, with its capitals in Samarkand and then Bukhara, was continuing the trade legacy of the Sogdians. Controlling the eastern end of the Iranian Plateau and Afghanistan, the Samanids had good relations with their neighbours, and this political stability kept trade flowing. Their merchants travelled far and wide, building a network of influence that reached even to Scandinavia. The Samanids also controlled rich silver mines; the coins they produced were popular all along the Silk Road.

During the ninth century, a group of Turkic tribes, including the Karluks, Yaghmas and Chigils – living around the Tian Shan mountains and the western end of the Tarim Basin near Kashgar – united to form the Karakhanid Khanate. In the mid-tenth century they converted to Islam, captured Kashgar and began to put pressure on the independent Buddhist kingdom of Khotan, which eventually led to a long war that was won by the Karakhanids in around 1006. Around this time, they also began a military campaign in Transoxiana, taking Isfijab, Ferghana, Ilaq, Samarkand and the Samanid capital, Bukhara. The Karakhanid conquest of the western Tarim Basin marked the beginning of the eventual Turkification and Islamification of the entire region.

By 874, the Tang, already beset by a series of natural disasters in the form of alternating floods and droughts, were engulfed in rebellions. First, a salt smuggler by the name of Wang Xianzhi gathered a thousand men and rose up in Changyuan in Henan province. The rebellion quickly spread and Wang was joined by Huang Chao, also a salt smuggler, who had raised a small army of his own. The rebellions resulted in the sacking of both Chang'an and Luoyang, and took a decade to suppress, severely weakening the Tang in the process. Bandit groups the size of small armies began to ravage the countryside, attacking merchant caravans and smuggling salt.

Another salt smuggler, Zhu Wen, who had served under Huang, helped Tang forces to defeat him and was rewarded with a series of military promotions. In 907, having reached the level of military governor, Zhu deposed Emperor Ai and took the throne for himself, thereby ending the Tang dynasty.

SONG DYNASTY

The fall of the Tang dynasty dealt trade along the Silk Road a significant blow, ushering in a period of more than 50 years of political turmoil before the beginning of the Song dynasty under the Emperor Taizu in 960. The return of stability brought an increase in both domestic and foreign trade.

When Taizu died in 976, his younger brother took the throne as Emperor Taizong. Keen to regain the territories in the north that were under the control of the breakaway state of the Northern Han and the Liao/Khitan Empire, a previously nomadic tribal confederation based in what is now Mongolia, Taizong personally led an army first against the Northern Han. Emboldened by the success of that campaign, he then took the army further north to attack the Khitan. That proved to be an unmitigated disaster, so much so that a Khitan counterattack came within a few days' march of the Song capital before being repulsed.

This demonstration of the Song lack of military strength led to a policy of appeasement. They inaugurated a tribute system – essentially an attempt to buy peace by making huge annual payments to the Liao/Khitan, the Jurchens in Manchuria, the Tanguts to the west and the Mongols in the north. With a healthy economy to back it up, the policy created a stable political environment that saw domestic and international trade thrive. The Chinese government also relaxed restrictions on commercial activities, allowing private trade to expand significantly. New marketplaces sprang up away from official government markets. The flowering of trade, in turn, led to the formation of trade unions and professional guilds; merchants began to specialize in either wholesale or retail sales. Banking and credit systems emerged and became increasingly sophisticated, and paper money was introduced for use throughout the empire.

The sums involved in the tribute trade were enormous. The annual tribute paid by the Song to the Liao amounted to some 200,000 taels of silver (a tael was equivalent to about 35 g) along with 300,000 bolts of silk. However, the balance of trade was such that the Song mostly made the money back – Song exports typically exceeded imports by a large margin. Even when it came to trade with the Tanguts, from whom the Chinese bought 20,000 horses a year at 20 bolts of silk each, the Song usually came out ahead.

The Tibetan-speaking Tanguts controlled the region around the Hexi Corridor and thus Chinese access to the Silk Road. In the early years of the Song dynasty, they were content to be a tributary state, engaging in nomadic pastoralism and acting as middlemen in trade between Central Asia and China. However, in 1038, a new leader, Li Yuanhao, assumed the title of Emperor Zhao Yuanhao and created a new dynasty, the Western Xia. He quickly embarked on a campaign to conquer China, but it fizzled out six years later after the Chinese agreed to pay an annual tribute. Despite the fragile peace between the Xia and Song, the former's stranglehold on overland Silk Road trade was one of the reasons that the Song turned its attention towards the Maritime Silk Road.

In order to help stimulate overland trade, the Song set up supervised markets along its northern border. The Chinese traded large quantities of silk, paper, porcelain, lacquerware, jewellery and agricultural products such as tea, ginger and rice and other grains, receiving in return military horses, camels and sheep, as well as goods that had been transported along the Silk Road, including cotton textiles and silk brocade from India and Persia, weaponry, ivory, perfume, gems and incense. The Song also established monopolies over the production of commodities such as tea and salt and the importation of spices and incense, helping to boost government revenues. However, direct overland trade to China along the Silk Road began to decline, leading to a decrease in contact with Central and Western Asia and an increasing impression of Chinese geographical and cultural isolation from the rest of continental Asia.

In 1127, the Song court's policy of appeasement came back to haunt it, when the Jurchens, having noted the Song's military weakness, attacked and seized control of the capital, Kaifeng, forcing the Song court to relocate south to the Yangtze River delta, where it established its capital in Hangzhou in 1138. These events split the dynasty into two distinct periods: the Northern Song (pre-invasion) and Southern Song (post-invasion).

Having lost control of the territories north of the Huai River, and thus direct access to the overland Silk Road, the Southern Song dynasty turned even more to the Maritime Silk Road. China's major port cities, including Guangzhou, Quanzhou and Fuzhou, all located in the south, became increasingly prosperous as well as increasingly multinational, with Arab and Indian traders taking up permanent residence. Maritime trade helped to ensure that China's economy continued to thrive.

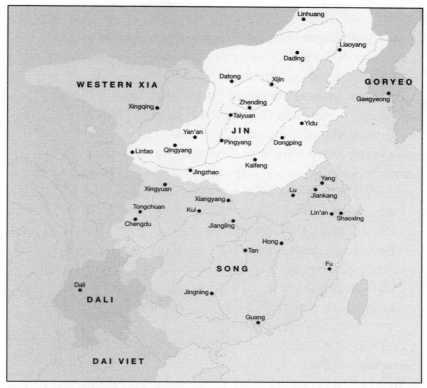

Post-invasion Southern Song territory in 1142, showing the northernmost third of China under Jin control.

Chang'an

Chang'an served as the capital of more than ten Chinese dynasties. As the Silk Road's eastern terminus, it became one of the world's great metropolises, home to large migrant communities and bustling markets, where cross-cultural fertilization was as important as mercantile exchanges.

The city's origins date back to the end of the second millennium BCE when the Western Zhou dynasty built its capital near Chang'an's eventual site. The Eastern Zhou moved the capital east to Luoyang (a common theme in Chinese history) but it returned to Chang'an in 202BCE under the Western Han dynasty.

Located just northwest of present-day Xi'an in Shaanxi Province, close to the Yellow and Wei rivers, the city was surrounded by mountains, which helped to protect it from invaders. Roads leading to Gansu, Sichuan, Henan, Hubei and Shanxi all converged there, and it was also at the end of the Hexi Corridor, which would become the main Silk Road route out of China.

In around 100BCE, the Emperor Wudi added several palaces and temples and created an imperial park. This was the period when the Silk Road officially opened and trade caravans regularly entered the city, which quickly became a cosmopolitan metropolis; by 2CE, it was home to about a quarter of a million people.

In 23CE, Chang'an was captured and sacked during a peasant rebellion. Two years later, the newly established Eastern Han dynasty moved its capital to Luoyang and Chang'an entered a long period of decline during which it was captured and almost destroyed by the Xiongnu. It later served as the capital for a number of small states during the Sixteen Kingdoms period, as well as the Wei, Zhou and Sui dynasties.

As capital of the Tang dynasty for three centuries from 618, Chang'an became one of the largest and most important cities in the world. Home to a diverse population of well over a million, it had a vast grid-pattern of streets, a complex administrative bureaucracy and an elegantly creative art world.

However, from the An Lushan Rebellion of 755 onwards it was sacked repeatedly and much of it was destroyed. In

763, it was briefly occupied by the Tibetan Empire and not long afterwards was besieged by Tibetan and Uighur Khaganate forces. It was again sacked and occupied during the Huang Chao Rebellion in 880, looted by the Tang forces that retook it, and then its citizens were slaughtered when Huang Chao took it back again. The city was attacked in 904–906 by the warlord Zhu Quanchong, at which point the capital once more moved to Luoyang – literally in this case, as many of its residents were relocated along with their wooden buildings – and Chang'an fell into disuse.

A que *(ceremonial tower) along the city walls of Chang'an, depicted in an eighth-century Tang-era tomb mural.*

In 1369, it was rebuilt to the southeast of its original location and renamed Xi'an ('Western Peace') after the Ming dynasty was established. Today, Xi'an is the capital of Shaanxi province and home to almost nine million people.

MONGOLS

At the beginning of the 13th century, several nomadic tribes were united under the leadership of Genghis (Chinggis) Khan, the son of a Mongol chieftain who was proclaimed ruler of the Mongols in 1206. Around this time, Central Asia's frigid, arid steppes were experiencing the mildest, wettest conditions in more than a millennium – ideal for raising the war horses and other livestock needed for an extended military campaign, which is exactly what Genghis initiated. His armies quickly dispatched the various kingdoms controlling northern China, before moving west into the settled areas of Central Asia, conquering Transoxiana and eastern Persia.

While this conflict initially disrupted trade along the Silk Road, once the nomads had vanquished their opponents, it quickly began to flow again. Genghis and the Mongols had a history of supporting trade. Foreign merchants, mostly Buddhist Uighurs, were provided with capital and protection under commercial partnerships known as *ortoq* agreements, which enabled them to carry out long-distance trade throughout Mongol-controlled lands. These arrangements were vital to the Mongols, providing information about neighbouring cultures as well as manufactured goods, of which the Mongols produced little themselves.

By the time Genghis died in 1227, the Mongol Empire stretched from the Pacific Ocean to the Caspian Sea, encompassing an area twice that of the Roman Empire at its height. Although he had besieged and then burnt to the ground the two vibrant trading cities

The world's largest statue of Genghis Khan, near Ulanbataar, Mongolia.

of Bukhara and Samarkand, the expansion of the empire across the Asian continent brought political stability to the region, ushering in the next great golden age of the Silk Road.

With Genghis gone, the empire began to fracture, as his sons and grandsons squabbled over succession and whether the empire should become sedentary and cosmopolitan or stay true to its steppe-nomad roots. Despite the disunity, the Mongols continued to expand their empire, capturing more of China and Persia, Tibet, the Caucasus, Russia, Ukraine and parts of Europe. They defeated the Abbasids, mercilessly sacking their glorious capital, Baghdad, in 1258, before continuing on to Syria, which proved to be the western limit for Mongol expansion in the Middle East.

The simmering disputes among the Mongols eventually led to civil war, with Kublai Khan, one of Genghis' many grandsons, eventually emerging as leader, although this didn't spell the end of internal divisions. In 1271, Kublai renamed the new Mongol regime in China the Yuan dynasty and moved his headquarters to Dadu (which would eventually become Beijing), while continuing his campaigns to wrest complete control of the country from the Song – which he achieved in 1276.

Thanks to continuing disagreement among the different branches of Genghis Khan's family, by the time of Kublai's death in 1294 the Mongol Empire had fractured into four separate khanates or empires: the Golden Horde in the northwest, the Chagatai Khanate in Central Asia, the Ilkhanate in the southwest and the Yuan dynasty in China. In 1304, the khanates agreed a peace treaty and accepted the supremacy of the Yuan emperor Temür, Kublai's grandson, although all four khanates still functioned as independent states.

The peace treaty ushered in a period of relative stability across Eurasia, the so-called *Pax Mongolica*. As in the Tang era, this stability led to a burgeoning of international trade and cultural exchanges between Asia and Europe. The Mongol Empire unified the trade networks that spread across northern Eurasia, connecting China, Central Asia, the Middle East and Eastern Europe into a single system, while also bringing to an end the Islamic Caliphate's dominance of global trade. Merchants were given tax exemptions and permission to use the empire's official relay stations; any losses incurred due to bandit attacks were repaid from the imperial treasury.

Marco Polo

In 1271, Marco Polo, a young Venetian born in around 1254, set off with his jewel-merchant father and uncle on a journey along the Silk Road and into the heart of the Mongol Empire. The elder Polos had earlier visited the court of Kublai Khan and had been asked by him to return to Europe and persuade the pope to send scholars to explain Christianity to him. Four years after they left Venice, they reached Kublai's summer court in Shangdu (also known as Xanadu) in Inner Mongolia.

Some 17 years later, the Polos started their return journey, initially accompanying a Mongol princess who was to become the consort of Arghun Khan in Persia. Begun in around 1292, it took them by sea to Sumatra, Ceylon (now Sri Lanka), southern India and the Persian Gulf, and then overland from Iran to Constantinople and on to Venice, arriving in 1295. Three years later, Marco was captured while taking part in a naval conflict between Venice and Genoa, and sent to prison, where his stories caught the attention of Rustichello, a writer from Pisa, who began to write them down. As Rustichello embellished many of the stories, the accuracy of the resulting book, published under a number of names including *The Million* and *Travels of Marco Polo*, is dubious at best, but it proved to be extremely popular, introducing Europeans to the fantastic world of the East. Following his release from jail, Marco returned to Venice, where he remained until his death in 1324.

Ibn Battuta

Often described as the world's first tourist, Muhammad Ibn Battuta was a Moroccan scholar who spent almost 30 years travelling widely around the medieval world. Born into a family of Islamic legal scholars in Tangier, Morocco, in 1304, he set off for the Hajj pilgrimage to Mecca at the age of 21, after completing his education. Travelling overland, he took an extremely meandering route with multiple diversions, visiting Alexandria, Cairo, Damascus, Hebron, Jerusalem, Bethlehem and Medina before finally arriving in Mecca in 1326. Then, rather than returning home, he kept travelling. His journey eventually took him across North Africa, the Horn of Africa, West Africa, the Middle East, Central Asia, Southeast Asia, South Asia and China, covering a distance of some 120,000 km (75,000 miles) and including about 40 present-day countries. He was attacked by bandits and pirates; worked as a judge in India and the Maldives, married and divorced several times; and met princesses, sultans, emperors and emperors. Towards the end of his life, he dictated an account of his travels, entitled *A Gift to Those Who Contemplate the Wonders of Cities and the Marvels of Travelling*. He died in 1368 or 1369.

But all good things must come to an end. In around 1330, an outbreak of the Black Plague took place in Asia – beginning in either western China or the steppe. It struck China's Hebei province in 1331; three years later, 90 per cent of the province's inhabitants were dead. The plague then spread westward along the Silk Road. Outbreaks followed in Persia and the Silk Road cities of Talas, Sarai and Samarkand, all of which are thought to have lost up to 70 per cent of their populations. In 1335, the plague claimed the ruler of the Ilkhanate, Abu Said, along with his sons and about 30 per cent of the Persian population. Because he left no appointed successor, Abu Said's death led to a fight over succession and the Ilkhanate began to break up into a series of small kingdoms ruled by a mixture of Mongols, Turks and Persians.

The Black Death's devastation wasn't over. From 1346 to 1353 it ravaged Europe, killing about half the population; an estimated 75–200 million people are believed to have died. Thought to have been carried west by Silk Road traders following both the overland and maritime trade routes, the plague reached the Middle East in 1347 – first Alexandria via Constantinople, then cities in what are now Lebanon, Syria and Palestine – causing further devastation. Mecca became infected in 1349.

Unsurprisingly, by causing significant depopulation, the plague led to an overall decline in global trade, including that along the Silk Roads. It also signalled an end to the period of political stability that Asia – and the Silk Road – had enjoyed as the Yuan dynasty, the Chagatai Khanate and the Ilkhanate all began to lose their grip on power.

Around the time that plague was breaking out in China, the country was struck by another natural disaster when widespread drought caused a devastating famine that killed as many as six million people. The disaster was widely interpreted as a sign that the Mongols had lost the 'Mandate of Heaven', and rebellions broke out across the country. Among the military leaders who arose during these was a peasant from Nanjing named Zhu Yuanzhang, who led an uprising and then built a unified army that drove the Mongols from China and back to Inner Mongolia. In 1368, he declared himself emperor of the new Ming dynasty, with its capital in Nanjing.

Zhu Yuanzhang, later known as Emperor Hongwu, became the first ruler of the Ming dynasty in 1368.

— 4 —
THE MARITIME SILK ROAD

Running in tandem with the overland Silk Road was a maritime trade network that eventually connected Asia, the Middle East, Africa and Europe. Like the overland Silk Road, the maritime network was a complex skein of links between ports in numerous different nations and regions. This Maritime Silk Road was arguably even more important for trade than its overland incarnation: it's thought that more silk and other goods were carried to the West along the Maritime Silk Road than along the overland routes.

The most frequently visited ports along the maritime trade routes grew into vibrant, wealthy coastal cities where goods and ideas were exchanged in bustling markets. Transient populations of merchants and sailors facilitated cultural exchanges; each ship that arrived into port brought both a valuable physical cargo and a wealth of knowledge and cultural peculiarities. Cities such as Alexandria, Muscat, Malacca, Guangzhou and Goa can all trace their history and prosperity to their positions on the Maritime Silk Road.

Trade routes encompassed the South China Sea, the Indian Ocean, the Bay of Bengal, the Arabian Sea, the Persian Gulf and Red Sea, and the Malacca Strait, stretching over 15,000 km (9,300 miles) from the west coast of Japan, past the Chinese coast, through Southeast Asia and past India to the Middle East and East Africa. Some of the most important routes linked Indian ports such as Barbarikon, Barygaza (modern day Bharuch) and Muziris with Middle Eastern ports such as Muscat, Sur, Kane and Aden on the Arabian Sea, and Myos Hormos, Muza and Berenike on the Red Sea. From the Middle East, goods could make their way on to the Mediterranean and Europe.

This 15th-century French miniature from Livre des merveilles du monde (Book of the Wonders of the World) *by Marco Polo and Rustichello, shows sailors navigating using a compass.*

Maritime traders typically exploited the seasonal monsoon (an Arabic word meaning 'season') winds, which carried boats across the Indian Ocean eastward to India in July, August and September and westward to the Middle East in December, January and February. Because early sailors were at the mercy of monsoon winds, they were often forced to spend lengthy periods in port, waiting for them to change direction with the changing seasons. This both enhanced the prosperity of the ports, whose businesses provided the merchants with warehousing for their goods, and food and accommodation during their stay, and also increased opportunities for cultural exchange.

For traders, the maritime routes offered several advantages over their overland counterparts. For example, on overland routes traders

— TIMELINE —

C. 5000BCE	*People first take to the sea in boats in the Persian Gulf*
C. 3000BCE	*Maritime trade starts in the Arabian Sea*
C. 2000BCE	*Traders using the monsoon winds to sail between the Arabian Peninsula and India*
C. 1100BCE	*Traders sailing around the East China Sea route*
C. 60CE	Periplus of the Erythraean Sea *published*
240s	*China sends envoys to explore trading opportunities in Southeast Asia*
C. 500	*Rome loses control of the Red Sea ports*
700	*Maritime trading links first established between Arabia and China*
982	*First recorded trading contact between China and the Philippines*
1371	*Haijin ('sea ban') policy enacted, restricting Chinese maritime trade*
1405–33	*Zheng He makes seven expeditions around the Indian Ocean*
1497	*Vasco da Gama rounds the Cape of Good Hope*
1511	*Portuguese take control of Malacca and with it the Straits of Malacca*
1521	*Ferdinand Magellan sails from Spain to the Philippines*
1567	*Haijin policy relaxed*
1647	*Qing ruler reinstitutes the Haijin policy*
1727	*Legal trade in the South China Sea resumes*

had to pass through multiple territories, each of which typically extracted taxes on their goods. In contrast, a maritime trader could often buy goods in one port and transport them directly to another, paying a single port tax at their destination. Under favourable conditions, marine craft were also much faster than the plodding horse and camel caravans used by overland traders; although when conditions were less favourable, the maritime routes could be extremely dangerous and numerous ships were lost to storms and submerged reefs. And finally, ships were capable of carrying much larger loads than were beasts of burden, which became particularly important as goods such as porcelain and tea began to increase in popularity; by the tenth century, ships were typically capable of carrying loads that weighed about 1,000 times what a camel could bear and required far less human labour than would a Silk Road caravan.

The overland and maritime Silk Roads were interlinked physically – with goods along one being transferred to the other at bustling ports – but their fortunes sometimes moved in opposite directions: when conflict or other factors increased the danger or difficulties involved in traversing the overland routes, merchants turned to the sea. And when the overland Silk Road eventually fell into obscurity, the Maritime Silk Road continued to thrive.

BEGINNINGS

Archaeological evidence suggests that people were taking to the sea in boats in the Persian Gulf and Gulf of Oman by as early as the end of the sixth millennium BCE, and in the Red Sea not long after. By the third millennium BCE, small trading vessels were plying the coastal waters of the Arabian Sea, travelling among the small towns, villages and trading ports on the coastline that links Arabia to the Indian subcontinent.

Initially, these small-scale traders probably only ventured short distances from their home ports, but by the end of the second millennium BCE, Indian and Arab merchants were using the monsoon winds to travel across open sea. These early exchanges brought luxury goods such as frankincense and myrrh from the Arabian Peninsula to India and spices from Asia, including cinnamon from Sri Lanka and cassia from China, to the Middle East. Traders also made contact with coastal settlements in East Africa, with whom they exchanged basic foodstuffs and building materials.

The Spice Islands

An archipelago of more than 1,000 islands located in the Banda Sea, east of Sulawesi in modern-day Indonesia, the Moluccas (or Maluku Islands) were long known as the Spice Islands because they were the only place where nutmeg, mace and cloves were grown. They were first discovered by the outside world during the 14th century, when Arab traders began to visit.

During the early days of the spice trade, when it was mostly conducted overland, upon arrival in Venice (at the time the primary point of trade contact between Europe and the East) the spices' value might have risen by as much as 1,000 per cent, making control of the source potentially very lucrative. The Portuguese arrived in the archipelago in 1513, having recently annexed Malacca. They were followed, in the late 1500s, by the Dutch and the English. The Dutch – in the form of the Dutch East India Company (DEIC) – began to establish settlements on a few of the islands and were soon battling with the Portuguese for control of the archipelago, emerging victorious in 1667, by which time the DEIC was the richest private company the world had ever seen.

Today, the islands remain the world's top producers of cloves, mace, nutmeg and pepper.

At the same time, seagoing traders were developing a network in the Mediterranean involving the early Phoenicians, Egypt, Cyprus and Greece. The Phoenicians went on to become the greatest seafaring civilization of the ancient world, dominating maritime trade in the Mediterranean for most of the first millennium BCE.

Meanwhile, in the east, a wave of migration took place around 4000BCE from Taiwan and southern China into Southeast Asia and eventually into Polynesia, Melanesia and across the Pacific. This spread was facilitated by a fairly advanced boatbuilding technology, and when these people settled, they quickly began trading among themselves.

China itself was relatively slow to join these nascent maritime trade networks. Ancient and medieval China was primarily an agricultural society that focused on the land, with sea expeditions and maritime trade a rarity. However, by the time of the Shang dynasty, in the middle of the second millennium BCE, trade was taking place between China and parts of Southeast Asia. This mostly took the form of natural products such as ivory, rhinoceros horn, tortoise shells, pearls and birds' feathers, and while it would have mostly been overland, some of the goods were carried on small coastal vessels by Malay traders. The growing importance of maritime trade to China is reflected in the use of cowrie shells as a form of currency.

By the Zhou dynasty, in the 11th century BCE, China, Japan and Korea were trading with each other along what became known as the East China Sea route, whose origins are said to lie in the voyage of a Chinese sage named Jizi, sent by the Zhou court. Setting sail from Bohai Bay near the Shandong Peninsula, he crossed the Yellow Sea to Korea, where he taught the locals about agriculture and the secrets of sericulture (silk production), and silk reeling and weaving.

Jade jewellery was moving from Taiwan to Southeast Asia by the second half of the first millennium BCE, via an extensive sea-based trade network, and there was regular trade between India and the

Malay Peninsula. Indian artisans began to set up shop in coastal towns on the peninsula, where they made colourful glass beads for the local markets.

During the third and second centuries BCE, maritime trade networks expanded considerably. Chinese ships sailed as far as India and Sri Lanka, where they met Arab merchants; sea routes connected Alexandria to China; Arab and Indian dhows sailed down from the Red Sea to Sri Lanka; Indian dhows went as far as the Straits of Malacca, where they met Chinese junks. Korea had also become a player in the trade around the Yellow Sea, moving among ports in Japan and China, carrying goods further south to what is now Vietnam and travelling to the Moluccas (Spice Islands) and to eastern Java, where they took on loads of cloves, nutmeg and mace. The opening up of the overland Silk Road in the second century BCE further spurred growth of the maritime networks as goods carried overland to Indian ports then made their way by sea to other parts of India and Southeast Asia.

Burgeoning trade around the Arabian Sea brought interest from the region's ruling dynasties. During the third century BCE, the Hellenistic Seleucids and the Ptolemaic Kingdom fought to control access to Mediterranean ports and Red Sea routes to Arabia and India. At that time, the Arabs controlled trade in the Levant, both on land and at sea. From the Persian Gulf, they had access to Mesopotamia, from the Red Sea to the coast of northeast Africa, and from the Isthmus of Suez to Egypt and the Mediterranean.

The vibrant sea trade also helped to promote the growth of a number of ports in Roman Egypt – none more than Alexandria. By the time Ptolemy XI bequeathed Alexandria to the Romans in 80BCE, the city had grown rich on revenues from port duties. The Romans used it as a hub for trade with India, and it quickly grew to become the ancient world's most important commercial centre and its largest market for spices. Large quantities of Egyptian cotton and wheat were also moving by sea from Alexandria to Rome.

Muscat

Lying in a cove on the northeast coast of what is now Oman, Muscat overlooks the Gulf of Oman and the Straits of Hormuz. For centuries, it was one of the most important trading centres on the Maritime Silk Road, a vital staging point for merchants travelling up the Persian Gulf to Asia, east to India and the Indian Ocean, or west along the Arabian coast to Africa. Its strategic position made it a focus for invading powers wishing to control the lucrative sea routes.

People have been living in the area around Muscat since the sixth millennium BCE. Surrounded by the Hajar Mountains, the settlement was virtually inaccessible from the land. The natural shelter afforded by a crescent-shaped cove, as well as a good freshwater supply, made the site perfect for development as a port. As early as the first century CE, the Greek geographer Ptolemy referred to it as Cryptus Portus ('Hidden Port').

The old city of Muscat, once a major trading centre on the Maritime Silk Road, is now separated from the rest of modern Muscat by coastal mountains.

During the third century CE, Muscat was captured by the Sassanid Persians, before being conquered by Islamic forces during the seventh century. In 751, Oman's tribal factions began to consolidate; tribal skirmishes still took place, however, and at the end of the ninth century, during a period of outright civil war, Oman was overrun by the Abbasids of Baghdad.

Under the Abbasids, who had strong trade links to the Indian Ocean, Muscat's importance as a trading port grew, with ships travelling to and from India, China and East Africa, although even then, it was subordinate to the port of Sohar, located to the northwest. The Abbasids ruled until the 11th century, when they were forced out by an Omani tribe known as the Yahmads. Maritime trade – and Muscat with it – continued to prosper.

By the beginning of the 16th century, Portugal was increasingly aggressive in its attempts to become the dominant maritime trading nation. In 1507, Portuguese forces invaded Muscat, burning and looting the city, and killing most of its inhabitants. They built two forts and surrounded the city with a high wall, as well as constructing fortified outposts along the adjacent coast.

The Ottoman Turks soon began sending military expeditions against Portugal's outposts around the Arabian Sea and in 1546 they subjected Muscat to a naval bombardment. On two occasions – in 1552 and 1581–8 – they captured the city, but on both occasions Portugal retook it, before being forced out for good in 1650.

The 19th century saw Muscat's fortunes decline as a port. Now it is Oman's capital and once more a bustling metropolis, with a population of about 850,000.

Among the other Roman ports to thrive in this new trading environment was Myos Hormos on the Red Sea, which was connected to the Nile Valley and Memphis. Along with Berenice, Myos Hormos was one of the two main ports in Roman Egypt for trade with India and Africa. The Greek geographer Strabo reported that in around 25BCE, at least 120 ships were sailing to India from Myos Hormos each year.

Kingdoms involved in the maritime trade gained substantially from it. Many taxed merchants heavily, none more so than Rome, which levied a 25 per cent tax called the *tetarte* ('fourth') on goods entering the Roman Empire; this impacted particularly on Indian Ocean trade.

Further east, Han-dynasty China made contact with the Malay Peninsula. This narrow strip of land played a vital role in connecting the trade networks of the South China Sea to those of the Bay of Bengal and on to the coasts of the Indian Ocean, the Red Sea, the Persian Gulf and the African continent. Most ships passed through the Straits of Malacca – the narrow stretch of water that separates the Malay Peninsula and the Indonesian island of Sumatra. Whoever controlled the strait effectively controlled the spice trade, holding the power to levy taxes on ships plying the so-called Spice Routes and participating in trade themselves. Cities that overlooked the strait, including Palembang (the capital of Srivijaya) and, much later, Malacca, became rich and powerful on the back of this trade.

The downside to passing through the strait was the risk of piracy. For this reason, some traders chose to unload their cargo on the coast adjacent to the Isthmus of Kra, the narrowest part of the Malay Peninsula, and pay locals to transport it across to the far coast, where it was loaded onto a different ship to continue its journey. This practice led to the foundation of the settlement of Khao Sam Kaeo (in modern Thailand) during the fourth century BCE and saw it grow into a cosmopolitan hub that drew merchants and artisans from across Asia.

By the first century CE, ships were regularly crossing the Arabian Sea and the Bay of Bengal. Coastal ports and cities were growing as trading networks became busier and more profitable. It was around this time that a Greek merchant wrote a manual of sailing directions, known as a *periplus*, for the Red Sea region. The *Periplus of the Erythraean Sea* summarized what was known about ports and the trade products available in them and provides a fascinating snapshot of the thriving commercial trade at that time.

Malacca

Running between the Malay Peninsula and the Indonesian island of Sumatra, the Straits of Malacca (also spelled Melaka) acted as a vital maritime trade route for Southeast Asia from around the first century CE. By the middle of the first millennium CE, a number of entrepôts and feeder points were established on the peninsula's west coast and at the northern entrance to the straits.

The city of Malacca began life as a fishing village inhabited by the Orang Laut people. The port was established in around 1400 by Parameswara, the ruler of Temasek (now Singapore), who had taken refuge in the village following an attack by forces from the Javanese kingdom of Majapahit. Impressed by the site's characteristics – it was accessible in all seasons, had access to freshwater springs and was strategically located at the narrowest point of the straits – he decided to establish a port and kingdom there. Passing ships soon began to call in to take on food and freshwater supplies.

According to legend, while visiting a Malay fishing village at the mouth of the Bertam River (now the Malacca River), Parameswara stopped to rest under a tree. One of his dogs

*cornered a mouse-deer, which fought back and pushed the
dog into the river. Impressed by the deer's courage, and
taking it as a propitious omen of the weak overcoming the
powerful, Parameswara decided to found a city on that spot,
naming it Malacca after the type of tree under which he
was sitting.*

The port grew quickly to become the most prosperous
entrepôt in the Malay Archipelago, serving a mixture of
Arab, Persian, Gujarati, Tamil, Bengali, Japanese, Siamese,
Jewish and Chinese traders who sailed in on the monsoon
winds in search of spices. The influence of the Arab, Persian
and Indian merchants was such that Malacca soon became
an Islamic sultanate. For
protection, Parameswara
forged an alliance with
Ming China, and Admiral
Zheng He stopped there
on several of his voyages.

*A 1545 painting of Afonso
de Albuquerque, Viceroy
of Portuguese Indies. De
Albuquerque conquered
Malacca in the 16th century
and shattered the diplomatic
relationships of its trading allies,
ultimately leading to the port's
decline.*

Around the start of the 16th century, news of Malacca's success reached the Portuguese. In 1511, Afonso de Albuquerque, viceroy of the Portuguese Indies, arrived with an armada. After conquering the city on his second attempt, he ordered the construction of a near-impregnable fortress and took over control of access to the Straits of Malacca and of the local spice trade.

As the Malacca Sultanate was a tributary state and ally of the Ming, this act of aggression was condemned by China. Chinese traders boycotted Malacca, and other Asian merchants also began to favour other ports, such as Johor on the southern tip of the Malay Peninsula, which had been established by the last Sultan of Malacca on fleeing from the Portuguese. Consequently, Malacca began to decline.

Over the next 300 years, it was variously controlled by the Dutch, the British and, during World War II, the Japanese. During the post-war period, Singapore's rise, combined with heavy silting in the Malacca estuary, saw Malacca's importance as a port diminish. In 2008, Malacca's old town was inscribed on the World Heritage list.

With the maritime networks becoming increasingly well established, foreign influences spread. In particular, Indian traders were increasingly setting up trading colonies in distant lands. During the first century CE, in the Mekong Delta in what is now southern Vietnam and Cambodia, the ancient state of Funan became the first important Hinduized kingdom in Southeast Asia. A seagoing nation, it had trade relations with India as well as China but was markedly influenced by Indian culture. During the 240s – the Three Kingdoms period in China – the king of Wu sent a diplomatic mission south to investigate the kingdoms of Southeast Asia, with a view to increasing trade. The two envoys, Zhu Ying and Kang Tai, travelled by sea to Funan, where they discovered a thriving and prosperous kingdom carrying on a lucrative trade with India and Rome.

Southeast Asia was the point where the Indian and East Asian maritime trade routes converged – at the junction between the Indian Ocean and the South China Sea. As well as being important sources for spices, regions such as the Malay Peninsula and the Indonesian archipelago also became lucrative trade hubs. Across the Indonesian archipelago, the early sultanates, known as harbour principalities, became rich by monopolizing trade in particular goods and/or serving as way stations along established routes.

The ancient temple at Phnom Da, built in the 11th century, reflected the wealth and power of the kingdom of Funan in the Mekong Delta.

From the end of the fourth century, as the Western Roman Empire began to stutter and crumble, trade suffered. The empire had been a lucrative market, and as its focus turned to fighting off barbarian attacks and dealing with internal instability, that market collapsed. When the empire itself collapsed at the end of the fifth century, Rome lost control of the Red Sea ports, some of which were subsequently abandoned. In the aftermath, Indian traders focused their efforts on trade with Southeast Asia, where their influence grew.

Periplus of the Erythraean Sea

The *Periplus of the Erythraean Sea* is an ancient 'travel guide' for maritime merchants, describing navigation details and trading opportunities for the different ports known to its author at the time. *Periplus* is a Latinized word derived from the Greek *periplous*, which literally means 'a sailing-around'. While the Erythraean Sea is a Greek name for the Red Sea, to the ancient Greeks it referred to a much wider area, and the *Periplus* covers the Indian Ocean, the Persian Gulf, the Bay of Bengal and the Gulf of Aden.

It's unclear when the text was written, but it's thought to date to the mid-first century, probably around 60CE. The author, also unknown, is believed to have been a Greek merchant or ship's captain who had first-hand experience of the subjects and places about which he wrote. Written in Greek, the manuscript contains 66 short chapters, most of which are no longer than a paragraph.

No original versions of the *Periplus* are known to exist, but a copy made during the tenth century by a Byzantine scribe is held by Heidelberg University Library, and the British Museum also has a copy that dates from the 14th or 15th century.

'And for the King there are brought into those places very costly vessels of silver, singing boys, beautiful maidens for the harem, fine wines, thin clothing of the finest weaves, and the choicest ointments.'

The Periplus of the Erythraean Sea

PEAK AND DECLINE

The collapse of Roman power ushered in a new period of disruption and conflict along the overland Silk Road, and many merchants turned to the sea. This shift hastened the decline of the overland routes, while technological advances in navigation, astronomy and shipbuilding combined to make long-distance sea travel increasingly safe and practical.

Arab, Indian and Chinese traders extended and consolidated the extensive trade network that now connected China, Southeast Asia, the Straits of Malacca, India, Africa and the Middle East, and cities along China's southeast coast blossomed. Arab traders, in particular, established themselves in the Indian Ocean and South China Sea, beginning to trade directly with China. Meanwhile, Chinese ships could be found sailing in the Persian Gulf and Red Sea, into Persia, Mesopotamia (up the Euphrates River), Arabia, Egypt, and Ethiopia and Somalia in the Horn of Africa.

The establishment of the Tang dynasty in 618 saw China blossom again, bringing political stability and economic prosperity. Settlements around the East Asian trade network sent tributary missions to the Tang court in the hope of establishing diplomatic relationships with the region's largest power.

This period brought an influx of foreigners into China, setting up trade businesses. By the beginning of the ninth century, Guangzhou, at that time the largest port in China, had as many as 200,000 foreign residents, including Arabs, Persians, Indians,

Africans and Turks. Muslim traders established trading colonies that became known as *fanfang* ('foreigners' districts') in a number of Chinese ports, including Guangzhou, Yangzhou and the recently-established Quanzhou. By the middle of the ninth century, it's thought that tens of thousands of Muslims were living on China's southeast coast.

It wasn't all smooth sailing, however. During the An Lushan Rebellion, which began in 755, a mixture of Arab Muslim soldiers who had been enlisted to help put down the rebellion and Arab and Persian pirates and merchants burned and looted Guangzhou. In response, the Tang government raised import duties and shut the port for about 50 years; foreign vessels wishing to trade in southern China had to do so via Hanoi (in modern Vietnam).

The An Lushan Rebellion was a major uprising against the Tang dynasty, spanning the reigns of three Tang emperors. This 11th-century painting depicts Emperor Xuanzong of Tang fleeing Chang'an to escape the violence and find sanctuary in Sichuan.

Berenike

Located on the edge of Egypt's Eastern Desert, about 965 km (600 miles) south of modern Suez, near the border of Egypt and Sudan, the Red Sea port of Berenike spent 800 years as a thriving Maritime Silk Road trading hub, where goods from Europe, the Middle East, south Asia, sub-Saharan Africa and southern Arabia were exchanged, before being abandoned and swallowed up by the desert sands.

Founded in 275 BCE by Ptolemy II of Egypt, who named it for his mother, Berenike was initially established for the importation of elephants, gold and ivory from Africa. The port's importance to Silk Road trade peaked during the first century BCE, when it was a vital trans-shipment point for trade between India, Arabia and Upper Egypt. Estimates suggest that around this time, at least 120 ships carrying about 75 tonnes of goods sailed each year between India and Berenike and the other Red Sea ports. After a two-week trek across the Eastern Desert from the Nile, goods arrived at Berenike and were loaded onto ships that then sailed down the Red Sea and over the Indian Ocean to India, southern Arabia and coastal Africa.

Living conditions in the city were harsh, its inhabitants forced to contend with extreme heat, very low rainfall and plagues of insects, but those who endured became wealthy on the back of the highly lucrative spice and incense trade. At its peak, the port was extremely cosmopolitan: archaeologists working at the site have found inscriptions in 12 different languages, including Greek, Hebrew Coptic, Sanskrit and one that has yet to be identified, and it's clear that several different religions were observed. There is abundant evidence that Indian traders were active in the city from at least the early Roman period.

At some point during the third or fourth century, Berenike was abandoned, before being repopulated in the fifth century and finally silting up during the sixth century. The port's ruins were identified in 1818 by Italian archaeologist Giovanni Battista Belzoni, and since 1994 they have been undergoing extensive archaeological excavations. Among the finds are a pet cemetery containing the remains of 17 dogs and cats, a letter in which a mother complains that her son doesn't write to her as often as she would like, a detailed bill of sale for a donkey, and a large jar containing more than 7 kg (15 lb) of black peppercorns from southwest India that dates back to the first century CE.

By now, trade was burgeoning with settlements in East Africa. Around the eighth century, cats, chickens and rats appear to have arrived there by ship and by the end of the century, Chinese merchants were regularly visiting the port of Sufala on the East African coast, cutting out Arab middlemen. By the ninth century there was a thriving trade with Africa in slaves, ivory and ambergris.

During the Song dynasty (from 960), China consolidated its maritime power. This process was hastened at the beginning of the 12th century when the Song were forced to move south after an uprising and invasion by the Jurchen. With access to the overland Silk Road cut off, China turned to the Maritime Silk Road; fortuitously, the nation's major ports were almost all in the south. Increasing output of goods in southern China provided a further incentive for development of maritime trade, with merchants keen to penetrate new markets overseas.

The focus on maritime trade spurred on a period of technological advancement that saw Chinese craftsmen adapt the compass, originally developed during the Han dynasty, for use at sea. It

A model of the world's first compass, invented by the Chinese during the Han dynasty in 400BCE.

also created a need for more ships, and shipbuilding became a major industry. This, in turn, led to numerous innovations in boat construction, which made ocean travel safer.

China's maritime trade outstripped its overland trade for the first time as the Song court sent missions to encourage Southeast Asian traders to visit. Chinese ships became more common across the Indian Ocean and the Chinese even began to displace Indian and Arab merchants in the South Pacific.

In 982, the first recorded direct contact between China and the Philippines took place when Filipino traders arrived in Guangzhou, although it's thought that the Chinese had already been trading with Filipino merchants for some time. Soon afterwards, Chinese traders from what is now Fujian province began to make regular visits to the Philippines, to towns along the coasts of Luzon, Mindoro and Sulu, to buy natural resources from the jungle interior and sell goods from China and Southeast Asia.

Meantime, during the 11th century, the division of power in the Islamic world, between the caliphates in Cairo and Baghdad, had caused commercial activities in the Persian Gulf to decline. Several ports were abandoned as the flow of goods moved from the Gulf to the Red Sea.

By the beginning of the Ming dynasty, at the end of the 14th century, China was the world leader in naval technology. Its shipbuilders used a combination of home-grown innovations and technologies borrowed and adapted from other seafaring nations.

After ascending to the throne in 1403, the Yongle Emperor ordered that a great fleet of 3,500 ships be built. He made a court eunuch by the name of Zheng He its admiral and sent him on a mission to extend Chinese political influence in the Indian Ocean by encouraging leaders of various maritime states to pay tribute. Zheng set sail in 1405 and over the next 28 years he made a total of seven naval expeditions, visiting Southeast Asia, India, Sri Lanka, the Horn of Africa and Arabia. Along the way, he presented gifts of gold, silver, porcelain and silk, and returned to China with envoys from many states, along with some unusual tributary gifts, including giraffes, ostriches and zebras.

The ships that made up the fleet were the largest in the world at that time. Zheng travelled with tens of thousands of armed troops and wasn't afraid to use them, brutally suppressing pirates and waging a land war against the Kingdom of Kotte on Sri Lanka. Following the death of the Yongle Emperor in 1424, the missions ceased (apart from one final mission, during which Zheng died), signalling the end of China's maritime dominance.

These missions had actually represented the reversal of an isolationist policy established at the beginning of the Ming dynasty. The *haijin* (literally 'sea ban') forbidding all private maritime trade and coastal settlement in China was first enacted in 1371 by the Ming Emperor Hongwu, who hoped that it would halt Japanese piracy in the South China Sea. However, the policy proved to be completely counterproductive: piracy and smuggling thrived, mostly carried out by Chinese who had been dispossessed by the prohibitions. The ban significantly reduced the flow of goods out of China, creating new opportunities for Southeast Asian and Japanese traders, while simultaneously restricting the flow of goods into China, creating opportunities for smugglers.

Zheng He

Born into a Muslim family in Yunnan, China, in 1371, Ma He was about ten when he was captured by the Ming army, castrated and placed in servitude in the household of the emperor's fourth son, Zhu Di. The two became close and when, in 1402, Zhu Di took the throne by force and proclaimed himself Emperor Yongle, he made Ma He director of palace servants and changed his name to Zheng He.

Zhu Di was determined to control Indian Ocean trade, and soon after taking the throne he placed Zheng He in charge of the construction of thousands of ships and then made him commander of the fleet. Over the next 30 years, Zheng He conducted seven voyages across the eastern Pacific and Indian oceans, trading and collecting tribute on the emperor's behalf. The first voyage consisted of a fleet of 317 ships, carrying personnel, horses, grain, fresh water and 28,000 armed troops. The wooden ships were among the largest ever built: the nine-masted flagship was over 120 m (400 ft) long and carried hundreds of soldiers on four tiers of decks.

Zheng He is believed to have died during his seventh voyage, sometime between 1431 and 1433. After this, the emperor called a halt to the expeditions and the ships were left to rot.

'When we arrived at the foreign countries, barbarian kings who resisted transformation and were not respectful we captured alive, and bandit soldiers who looted and plundered recklessly we exterminated. Because of this the sea routes became pure and peaceful and the foreign peoples could rely upon them and pursue their occupations in safety.'

Commemorative inscription in
Liujia Harbour near Shanghai

Ironically, piracy all but disappeared when the policy was significantly watered down in 1567 after the Ming began to struggle with the loss of income from taxes on trade. Chinese merchants were then permitted to engage in foreign maritime trade, although their activities were still restricted.

By this time, the trading environment in Asia had altered significantly. During the late 15th century, the Portuguese explorer Vasco da Gama rounded the Cape of Good Hope, the southern tip of Africa. European sailors were now connected with Southeast Asian maritime routes for the first time, initiating direct European involvement in the spice trade. By the 16th and 17th centuries, the Portuguese, Dutch and British were fighting for control of the maritime routes through Asia and the associated trade. In 1511, the Portuguese occupied Malacca, giving them control of the Straits of Malacca, and, six years later, they began trading directly with the Chinese via Guangzhou. They were soon expelled, but were permitted to settle in Macao in 1557 after helping the Chinese to suppress piracy.

European activity was further extended when, in 1521, Ferdinand Magellan sailed from Spain to the Philippines via an eastern route, the first time Europeans had reached the archipelago. Although he was killed there, one of his ships managed to return to Spain with a cargo of spices from Indonesia. Spanish plans to turn the Philippines into a source of spices were stymied by unsuitable growing conditions, but they soon discovered the potential for trade. In 1571, Spanish sailors rescued the crew of a sinking sampan and transported them to China; the following year, the Chinese expressed their gratitude by sending a trading vessel loaded with silk, porcelain and other Chinese goods to Mexico, whence its cargo was transported to Spain. There, the goods found an eager market. Manila quickly became the hub for a trade network that funnelled goods from Southeast Asia, Japan, Indonesia, India and especially China to Europe, with about 30 or 40 heavily laden junks arriving in the Philippines from China each year. The trans-Pacific trade route along which these goods flowed to Europe was jealously guarded by Spain.

By the beginning of the 17th century, the Dutch had consolidated their hold over the spice trade in the Indonesia archipelago. The Dutch East India Company had set up a number of permanent trading posts, but their activities were restricted by conflict with the Portuguese and the British.

In 1647, the Qing regent Prince Rui resumed the *haijin* policy, followed by an even more severe version, instituted in 1661. Coastal residents in several Chinese provinces were forced to destroy their properties and move inland by about 20 km (12 miles), ships were destroyed and foreign trade was only permitted through Macao. The ban was lifted and reimposed several times during the 17th and 18th centuries, and Chinese traders emigrated in huge numbers; the Chinese immigrant community in Jakarta was estimated at 100,000 during the 18th century. Legal trade in the South China Sea resumed in 1727, but by this time the trading environment was very different, with European involvement shifting the balance. In 1757, the Qianlong Emperor declared that Guangzhou was to be the only Chinese port open to foreign traders.

The restrictions on trade eventually precipitated the First Opium War between China and the British. The 1842 Treaty of Nanking,

A 16th-century depiction of two pre-colonial nobles in the Philippines who were known as the Tagalog Maginoo. The Spanish commissioned many such depictions for the Boder Codex, *a colonial record of the native society at the time.*

which marked the war's end and saw the opening of four new ports in China, is generally considered to have ended China's isolation, but legal trade was still limited to the five specified ports. By this stage, the Maritime Silk Road had effectively been subsumed into what had become a global maritime trade network.

DANGERS

Although maritime trade could be very lucrative, voyages along the Maritime Silk Road were extremely dangerous. Maps were rudimentary at best, so hidden reefs were a constant threat, and shipbuilding technology was such that the ships often weren't very seaworthy, so were unable to withstand bad weather.

During the early years, one of the most significant threats to sailors was lack of drinking water. Navigation techniques and technology were poorly developed, and ships were largely at the whim of the elements, so journeys often lasted longer than expected as vessels were blown off course. Supplies of food and water were inadequate to cope with the added duration. The growth of ports along the trade routes thus improved safety by increasing the opportunities to stop and take on fresh supplies.

As maritime trade became more lucrative, it inevitably attracted pirates. Chinese sources suggest that pirates were active in local waters as early as the fifth century BCE and ancient Roman accounts describe the waters of the western Indian Ocean as being 'very greatly infested by pirates'. In southern India, governments were often forced to intervene to reduce the impact of piracy. In 828, during the Silla Kingdom period, a Korean general established Cheonghaejin, a military base-cum-trading hub, on Wando island, with the joint aims of trading with China and Japan and protecting Silla merchant fleets from pirates.

As trade ebbed and flowed, so too did the pirate scourge; piracy flourished as Asian sea trade boomed between the tenth and 13th centuries. Japanese pirates were an important factor in ordering East Asia's maritime world during the 15th and 16th centuries,

A contemporary silk painting shows the notorious 17th-century pirate Zheng Chenggong. He made his fortune in trade and piracy, and his legacy was to establish Chinese control over Taiwan. He is regarded as a hero even today.

while Chinese piracy reached a peak during the 17th century, when pirate bands could number in the tens of thousands. The power of these pirate leagues far surpassed that of the Chinese imperial navy and they became formidable regional powers in their own right, even forming alliances with foreign powers. In 1661, the pirate lord Zheng Chenggong (also known as Koxinga) declared himself 'sea king'. His forces drove the Dutch from Taiwan and controlled the island for the next 20 years.

In order to mitigate all of these risks, investors typically had small stakes in a number of different ships. Hence each ship was bankrolled by a number of different investors.

— 5 —
THE END
OF THE ROAD

During the late 14th century, Eurasia was slowly beginning to recover from the scourge of the Black Death. At the same time, the Mongol Empire was disintegrating and the political, cultural and economic unity of the Silk Road was starting to unravel. As the empire's vast territory split up into independent kingdoms, customs tariffs, tolls and inspections increased, making goods much more expensive. The routes also became more unsafe, as banditry and petty warfare increased.

TIMURID CONNECTIONS

Into the breach stepped the Turco-Mongol conqueror Timur (also known as Tamerlane), who reconquered many of the regions that had made up the western Mongol Empire and established his own Timurid Empire in around 1370. He made the great trading city of Samarkand his capital and set about restoring it to its former glory, initiating extensive building works, many of which were aimed at rejuvenating trade. Timur wanted to make Samarkand the most beautiful city in the world, a glorious and enduring manifestation of the might and power of his empire. This quest for beauty and luxury in itself helped to rejuvenate trade in Central Asia, as caravans came from China and the Middle East to supply furs, silk, jewels and porcelain to the city's elite.

Timur also hoped to reactivate the Silk Road and monopolize trade between Europe and China by destroying any trade routes that bypassed his territory. Through redirecting all regional trade to land that he controlled, he hoped to rebuild and rejuvenate cities

The great conqueror Timur (1336–1405) established the Timurid Empire in Central Asia and Persia. He went to war against the Golden Horde in order to stimulate his part of the Silk Road. In this miniature painting he is shown surrounded by his successors and descendants.

laid low by years of Mongol and nomad rule. In order to achieve this, he took on the so-called Golden Horde, the largest of the khanates formed after the death of Genghis Khan; the Delhi Sultanate, which ruled India at the time; and Turkey's Ottoman Empire.

The Golden Horde controlled territory from Siberia to Eastern Europe, through which the most northerly routes of the Silk Road passed. Timur launched a war against the khanate, sacking the trading cities of Astrakhan (in the Volga River delta in modern Russia) and Sarai Berke, the Golden Horde's capital (modern Kolobovka, also on the Volga), in 1395, as well as destroying Crimean trade centres and deporting the most skilful craftsmen to Samarkand. Caravans carried plundered artworks and other treasures back to the capital.

By effectively closing off the most northern routes, Timur achieved his aim: the caravan trade transferred south. Customs duties and taxes were raised in the caravan cities along the route and

– TIMELINE –

1370 *Start of Timurid Empire (1370–1404)*

1405 *Death of Timur*

1448 *Oirats overrun Hami, shutting off Chinese access to the Silk Road*

1453 *Ottomans conquer Constantinople, ending the Byzantine Empire*

1497 *Vasco da Gama rounds the Cape of Good Hope, connecting Europe to Southeast Asia*

1507 *End of the Timurid Empire*

1513 *Moghuls overrun Hami, shutting off Chinese access to the Silk Road*

1552 *Kazan and Astrakhan khanates annexed by Russia*

1634 *Start of Dzungar Khanate*

1644 *Start of the Qing dynasty*

1689 *Treaty of Nerchinsk establishes a common border between Russia and China*

1690 *Start of the Mughal Empire*

the various provinces through which it passed were held responsible for the safety of merchants who travelled through them, forced to pay double the value of any losses sustained to the deprived merchants and to pay five times the value to Timur. Unsurprisingly, security along the Silk Road increased – indeed, crime practically disappeared.

Timur also spent significant funds on improving the infrastructure along the trade routes, building military posts, bridges, horse relay stations and caravanserais, and even went so far as to bail out struggling merchants by lending them money. The routes all converged on Samarkand and the city enjoyed a new golden age as it reaped the benefits flowing from its position at the crossroads of Asia. Large caravans of as many as 800 camels travelled between Samarkand and Beijing, the journey taking about a year – much longer than it would have taken during Genghis Khan's reign.

Two years before the beginning of the Timurid Empire, the Hongwu Emperor had ascended to the throne in China, marking the start of the Ming dynasty and the end of the Mongol Yuan dynasty. At the time, relations between China and Central Asia were unsettled. In response to the humiliation of Mongol rule, the Ming became dominated by nationalism and a desire to rediscover China's cultural heritage. The country once again turned inwards, and distrust of foreign powers grew. In contrast to the all-inclusive commercial policies of the Mongol era, the emperor adopted a policy of semi-isolation, placing restrictions on tribute and trade relations with foreign states.

However, he still needed to maintain contact with China's neighbours, particularly along the northwestern frontiers and in the distant Central Asian regions. So, early in his reign, the emperor sent envoys to many of the kingdoms formerly controlled by the Mongols to announce that the Ming should now be recognized as the regional ruler. In 1395, an embassy of 1,500 Chinese led by three envoys reached Samarkand. Timur was enraged by the letter they handed him, which used language suggesting he was a mere Chinese vassal, and had the embassy imprisoned, while also making plans to invade China. In 1405, he set out to do just that, reasoning that by conquering China he could take control of the eastern end of the Silk Road. However, by this time he was almost 70 years old and too weak even to walk. In little more than a month, he fell ill and died, and the campaign was abandoned.

Following Timur's death a struggle for the succession broke out.

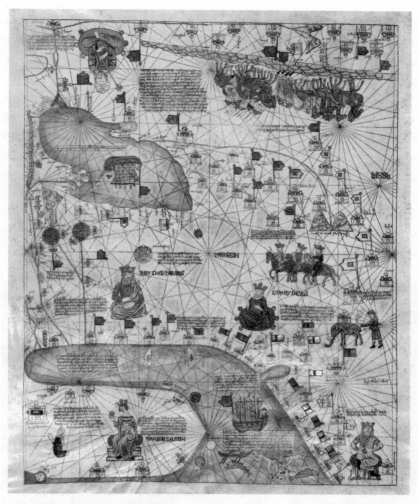

A map from the Catalan Atlas *(1375) shows the Aral Sea, the Volga River, the Caspian Sea, the Caucasus, the Euphrates River, the Arabian Peninsula and the cities of Delhi, Mecca, Baghdad, Samarkand and Astrakhan. This Central Asian region was also the centre of the Timurid Empire, which sought to control the trade of the Silk Road.*

One of his sons, Shahrukh Bahadur, eventually became ruler of the Timurid domains and made Herat in modern Afghanistan his capital. More interested in trade than territorial expansion, Shahrukh sent an embassy to China, the first of many; between 1408 and 1413, the Timurids sent nine embassies to the Ming court, offering horses, jade and exotic animals including leopards and lions, and receiving silk and other luxuries in return.

China remained keen to develop and consolidate trade relations with Central and western Asia, particularly as it required large numbers of high-quality militarily capable horses in order to stand up to the menace posed by the newly organized remnants of the Mongol Empire. Hence, in response to the Timurid overtures, the third Ming emperor, Yongle, sent a mission led by a much-travelled diplomat named Chen Cheng to the Timurids in 1414. On his return the next year, Chen presented to the court a report on his journey, which focused on the economic practices he had observed,

This ceramic door frame tile from the Porcelain Pagoda comes from the time of the Yongle Emperor (1403–1424). His efforts established open trade between China and the Timurid Empire.

providing useful tips for merchants seeking to foster trade with Central Asia. He returned to Herat in 1417, where he again met with Shahrukh as well as his son Ulugh Beg, the governor of Samarkand. He brought with him a letter from the Chinese court that called for open trade and tribute relations between the two empires, as well as gifts of silver, silk, brocades, falcons and porcelain. Soon, merchants from the Timurid territories were transporting locally made fabrics and luxuries, horses and camels to the Ming and returning with silk fabric, porcelain, silver, mirrors and paper.

The Timurids also enjoyed strong trade connections with India. Exchanges took place via the two commercial hubs of Kabul and Kandahar, now in Afghanistan. The Indians were interested in horses – like the Chinese, they needed them for transportation and military purposes but were unable to produce them in sufficient numbers domestically – and as many as 10,000 Central Asian horses were brought to Kabul each year. From Hindustan came slaves, white fabrics, sugar, dyestuffs and medicinal ingredients.

By the early 15th century, relatively secure long-distance trade routes connecting all the Eurasian civilizations of the time had been established in a network that converged on the Middle East. However, the peace and security were not to last. In the early 1400s, a Mongol confederation known as the Oirats rose to power and began to put pressure on China's northern and northwestern borders. From the 1430s, they conducted raids on the trade routes linking what are now Xinjiang and Gansu, and in 1448 they overran the oasis town of Hami in the Tarim Basin annexed by China in 1404, forcing the Ming out of their gateway to Central Asia and taking control of a key section of the Silk Road. Then, in 1449, they captured the Ming Emperor himself at the Battle of Tumu near the Great Wall, before returning him four years later. In response, the Ming began a grand project to reconstruct and fortify the Great Wall. Not long afterwards, internecine squabbling saw the Oirat Empire collapse.

Central Asian horses were important for transportation and military purposes. This watercolour depicts horsemen assembling outside the city of Kabul, Afghanistan.

Samarkand

Located in the Zerafshan Valley in what is now northeastern Uzbekistan, Samarkand is one of the oldest cities in Central Asia. Thanks to the prosperity that flowed from its position at the junction of trade routes to China, India and the Mediterranean, it became one of the greatest Silk Road cities.

Settlement in the region dates back to 1500BCE, but it's thought that the city was founded between the eighth and seventh centuries BCE. From its early days, the area was inhabited by the Sogdians, a people of Iranian origin who were renowned as traders across Central Asia. When Sogdiana was annexed by the Persian Achaemenid Empire during the sixth century BCE, Samarkand became a provincial capital, growing into a substantial city renowned for craft production.

112

In 329BCE, the city was captured and extensively damaged by Alexander the Great. However, it quickly recovered under its new Hellenic rulers, who used its Greek name, Marakanda. Following Alexander's death, Samarkand became part of various Greek successor states before undergoing a period of decline until the fifth century. It was then ruled by a seies of Iranian and Turkic leaders.

Chinese troops invaded Central Asia in 751, to be defeated by an army led by Samarkand's Abbasid governor, Abu Muslim. Among the more than 20,000 Chinese soldiers taken prisoner were some who knew the secrets of papermaking. Before long, Samarkand had become the first Muslim hub for paper manufacture.

At the end of the ninth century, the Abbasids were replaced by the Samanids, who bolstered the city's position as a trading centre. In around 1000, they were overthrown by the Karakhanids and over the next two centuries Samarkand was ruled by a succession of Turkic tribes.

It was again invaded and largely destroyed in 1220, by the Mongols, but was quickly rebuilt. Samarkand's citizens revolted against Mongol rule in 1365 and not long afterwards, Timur made the city his capital, initiating a period of construction that began with the building of a central shop-lined street aimed at encouraging trade. He also forcibly recruited artists, craftsmen, architects and merchants from conquered territories, eventually making Samarkand Central Asia's main economic and cultural centre.

Following Timur's death, his successor, Shahrukh, moved the imperial capital to Herat (in modern Afghanistan) and made his 16-year-old son, Ulugh Beg, governor of Samarkand. Keen to turn the city into an intellectual centre, Ulugh Beg built a university and a great observatory.

In 1500, the city was incorporated into the Khanate of Bukhara. The period of decline that followed saw it completely depopulated from the 1720s to the 1770s. Today, however, Samarkand is Uzbekistan's second-largest city, with a population of more than half a million. The city's historic quarter was designated a UNESCO World Heritage site in 2001.

The Registan (public square) in the ancient city of Samarkand is framed with three madrasahs, or educational institutions.

In China itself, power had been eroded by the end of the 15th century through a series of unsuccessful military campaigns, corruption and demoralization among the military and loss of tax revenues through evasion. Such was the deterioration that the imperial court attempted to limit the number of trade and tribute missions arriving from the northwest because of the cost. With distant nations' envoys and traders both deterred from travelling to China, business along the overland Silk Roads reached its lowest point for millennia.

This didn't go down well in some of the Tarim Basin oases, and the region became more turbulent as China's relations with Central Asia went from cooperation to conflict. In 1513 the Moghuls, under Mansur Khan, ruler of Turfan, marched into Hami and the city was lost to the Ming for the remainder of the dynasty. However, Moghul rule over the northern Tarim Basin worked to improve trade, as it brought to an end the political squabbling among the regions' powers.

Meanwhile, in 1453, Constantinople, and with it the Byzantine Empire, had fallen to the Turkish Ottoman Empire, which thereby gained control of the western end of the Silk Road. According to some scholars, this led to the closure of the Silk Road, as the Ottomans cut ties with Europe. However, others suggest that the consolidation of the Ottoman and Iranian Safavid empires in the Middle East actually led to a revival of overland trade – albeit frequently interrupted when the two empires went to war with each other – by opening up new Mediterranean markets through which European merchants could buy Asian exports.

At the end of the 15th century, the Portuguese explorer Vasco da Gama arrived in India, having opened up a sea route between Europe and Asia and hastened the decline of the overland routes. By this stage, the Persians had mastered the art of sericulture, severely weakening the Chinese monopoly on silk and reducing the volume of trade in the material. The secrets of silk production were known as far away as Europe; Lyon in France was manufacturing quantities of silk and supplying a large part of the European market. This all led to a significant decrease in the revenue generated by Silk Road trade.

By the early 16th century, the Timurid empire was collapsing. Persia, the Caucasus, Mesopotamia and Eastern Anatolia fell to the Safavid dynasty, while Muhammad Sheibani, a nomadic Uzbek tribal leader, conquered Samarkand, Herat, Ferghana and Bukhara, setting up the Khanate of Bukhara under the Shaybanid dynasty. While Bukhara had long been a hub for trade, under Shaybanid rule it entered a golden age; most of the city's most celebrated and striking monuments date from this period. The Shaybanids controlled a large part of Central Asia, covering much of the modern-day '-stans', which allowed Bukhara to grow rich on trade revenues as well as gaining a reputation as a spiritual and cultural centre. Trade caravans were sent far and wide, visiting Moscow, India, Iran, Kashgar, Siberia and the Kazakh steppe.

Diasporic communities were settling throughout the region, with many of their members acting as traders, merchants, moneylenders. Armenian merchants from the Safavid Empire travelled north into Russia and Central Asia, and west into the Ottoman Empire, settling as far away as the Netherlands, while also establishing outposts throughout the Mediterranean. Indian merchants travelled across the Caspian Sea to Astrakhan and through the Ferghana Valley into Central Asia. The Bukharans travelled east into China and northwest into Russia, which was now becoming an increasingly important player in Eurasian trade.

Isfahan

Renowned for its beauty, Isfahan was once one of Central Asia's largest and most important cities. Positioned on a Silk Road crossroads in what is now central Iran, its prosperity sprang from its role as a trading hub. Such was its splendour that it became the subject of an Iranian proverb: 'Isfahan is half the world.'

The city's origins date back to the Elamite civilization of the second and third millennia BCE. By the time of the Achaemenid Empire in the sixth century BCE, it was both religiously and ethnically diverse, a tradition of tolerance that continued under the Parthians. Their successors, the Sassanids, brought political decline, but when Isfahan was captured by the Arabs in 642 it became a provincial capital and grew prosperous. It then saw further prominence during the 11th and 12th centuries as capital of the Seljuk Empire. The Seljuks introduced a new, uniquely Iranian style of architecture, constructing numerous large mosques with unprecedentedly spacious domed chambers.

The Friday Mosque in Isfahan is one of the oldest mosques in Iran. It was built in the eighth century, then rebuilt in the 11th century during the Seljuk dynasty.

However, it was in 1598 that Isfahan entered its golden age, when the Safavid ruler Shah Abbas I made it his capital. He commissioned a series of major building works, rebuilding the city into one of the largest and most beautiful of its time. This period saw construction of many of the monuments and buildings for which Isfahan is renowned today, including a new *maidan* (city square), among the world's largest, and several impressive mosques. Entrance gateways, domes, minarets and some interior spaces were decorated with brightly-coloured tiles, a style that became characteristic of Iranian architecture and reached its zenith in Isfahan.

Shah Abbas I recognized the importance of trade and effectively rerouted the Silk Road through the city in order to gain a trade monopoly. He also instituted a programme of infrastructure development to facilitate trade, building bridges, roads and caravanserais. Traders were accommodated in a new market, the Imperial Bazaar, built where the Great Bazaar – a winding 2-km (mile-long) covered street connecting the old and new *maidan*s – met the new *maidan*. As well as shops and workshops, the Imperial Bazaar contained the state mint, a hospital, a public bath and a caravanserai.

During the 16th and 17th centuries, many European merchants settled in Isfahan. They were joined by hundreds of thousands of deportees and migrants from the Caucasus, including Georgians, Circassians, Dagestanis and Armenians. Today, Isfahan is Iran's third-largest city, with a population of roughly two million. It boasts two World Heritage sites: the Friday Mosque and Naqsh-e Jahan Square.

RUSSIA AND THE QING

The Russian tsar, Ivan the Terrible, annexed the Kazan and Astrakhan khanates in 1552, giving Moscow direct access to Central Asia. Six years later, Anthony Jenkinson, a British traveller and agent of the Muscovy Company and the English crown, acting as a representative of Ivan the Terrible, visited Bukhara to discuss trade. On his return to Moscow the following year, he was accompanied by envoys from Bukhara, Balkh and Urgench. Russian merchants and envoys began to make frequent visits to the region, trading and scoping out trade routes to China. Jenkinson, meanwhile, established a profitable trade in spices and silk between Persia, Russia and England, with up to 100,000 kg (220,000 lb) of Persian raw silk travelling to Russia each year. Russia went on to defeat the Siberian Khanate in 1598, then set about expanding eastwards, establishing a series of Siberian outposts that allowed Russian, Tatar and Bukharan merchants to rely on the Russian state to protect trade caravans moving between China and Europe.

In 1644, military forces from Manchuria (now northeastern China) occupied China, establishing the Qing dynasty, which was to be the last of China's imperial dynasties. The Manchus were a semi-nomadic people descended from a group called the Tungus.

One of their first orders of business was dealing with the Dzungar Khanate, an Oirat khanate on the Eurasian steppe that had formed in 1620. The last major nomadic empire created after the break-up of the Mongol Empire, it ultimately controlled a region stretching from the western end of the Great Wall to present-day Kazakhstan, and from present-day Kyrgyzstan to southern Siberia. In 1680, Galdan, the fourth son of the khanate's founder, led 100,000 cavalry into the Tarim Basin, which was eventually entirely occupied and incorporated into the Dzungar empire. Although the Dzungars sent twice-yearly tribute missions to Beijing to exchange furs and horses for silk and cotton textiles, military tensions with the Qing were ever-present. These began to come to a head in 1696. After cutting off trade with the Dzungars, the Qing sent a 400,000-strong army to what became known as Outer Mongolia, where they crushed their Dzungar opposition, annexing the region. Two years later, the Manchus also reoccupied Barkoel and Hami.

Dzungar depredations had an unsettling effect on Central Asia. For example, after the nomads moved into what is now Kazakhstan, many Kazakhs moved west and north towards the Russian border. There they took over control of key trade routes that linked the tsardom to Central Asia. Increasingly, they took on roles as caravan guides while also trading in towns along the frontier.

During the first half of the 18th century, the Qing worked to improve supply lines, trade and security along the Hexi Corridor between China and Central Asia, setting up garrisons of 200–1,000 troops in strategic sites near sources of water, fodder and wood. These garrisons were used for grain and weapons storage but also as focal points for farming settlements that would hopefully provide grain to feed the troops manning them.

With the Russian empire moving eastwards and the Qing dynasty expanding to the north, it was inevitable that the two nations would bump up against each other. By the late 17th century, they were working to create a common border, which eventually led to the signing, in 1689, of the Treaty of Nerchinsk.

Soon Russian merchants began organizing caravans from Nerchinsk to Beijing, a round trip that usually took about a year. However, Tsar Peter the Great decided that the state should have a monopoly on trade, and between 1697 and 1722, 14 Russian state caravans made their way to Beijing. Although private trade continued, it typically only travelled short distances. Russia was particularly keen to sell furs, a potential source of generous revenues, to China – the world's largest market. Russian demand for tea was also a key driver of trade: grown in southern China, it was processed into bricks that made the lengthy journey to Russia on camelback.

From 1717, the Chinese began to push for further delineation of the border, and in 1722 they blocked trade until the issue was settled. In 1727, Russia and China signed the Treaty of Kyakhta, which further specified the boundary, while also setting out terms of trade. All official trade was to pass through points near Kyakhta and Tsurukaitu on the border, and caravans would be three years apart. There were six state caravans from Kyakhta between 1727 and 1760. The first carried almost 300,000 roubles' worth of goods, including 2,100,000 furs. It returned with 125,000 m (410,000 ft) of silk, 570,000 m (1,870,000 ft) of cotton, 13,600 kg (30,000 lb) of tea, 65,000 roubles in gold and silver and 404,000 unsold pelts, which were then bartered at the border. In 1762 the Russian empress Catherine the Great replaced state caravans with free trade; Russian goods would be sold or bartered at Kyakhta.

The opening up of this Siberian Road between Moscow and

Beijing represented another alternative, besides the Maritime Silk Road, to the overland Silk Road for moving products between Europe and China. From the second half of the 17th century to the first half of the 18th century, Central Asia was regularly engulfed in warfare, so the Siberian route prospered.

From the end of the 17th century, trade increasingly bypassed the various kingdoms and settlements in Central Asia as it shifted to the Maritime Silk Road and the Siberian Road. The consequent loss of income from customs duties was catastrophic for many, as it was their main source of revenue, relied on to defend territory, maintain security on the trade routes and repair irrigation canals and otherwise support agriculture in what was a brutal farming environment. Many rulers attempted to use warfare to shore up their revenues, leading to an increase in turmoil and creating a vicious circle whereby the region became even less attractive to long-distance traders, resulting in further contraction of trade.

Keen to secure their borders, the Qing kept up their military operations along the Silk Road. By the middle of the 18th century, they had decisively subdued the Dzungar Khanate and annexed the Taklamakan region, creating the basis of present-day Xinjiang province. This once more gave China full control of the Western Regions.

The Manchus were still very keen on the large, powerful Central Asian horses, which formed the backbone of their cavalry. Each year in late summer, Kazakh traders would arrive at the Chinese frontier at the foot of the Tian Shan, where special trade fairs were set up. There the Kazakhs, as well as Kyrgyz nomads, would exchange horses (3,000–4,000 per year) and other livestock for bolts of silk, metal utensils, cotton cloth, brick tea and porcelain, trading with merchants from China who were often working on behalf of the military.

In the second half of the 18th century, Qing success in the Western Regions led to diplomatic border agreements and tariff regimes with various neighbouring Central Asian peoples and states. This period of regional peace, lasting until the early 19th century, saw something

Tuyoq or Tuyugou or Tuyuk is an ancient oasis-village in the Taklamakan desert, 70 km (43 miles) east of Turpan in a lush valley cutting into the Flaming Mountains in the Xinjiang Uighur Autonomous Region of China.

of a recovery in trade and economic prosperity on much of the Silk Road. The Chinese authorities upgraded the trade routes, installing roadside inns and water depots. In 1773, a high-ranking Qing dignitary named Wen Shou who visited a number of oasis towns on China's new frontier, described shops clustered 'as closely as the teeth of a comb' along market streets and pedlars crowding the roads.

During this phase, Bukhara continued to function as an important trade hub, where goods from India (textiles, medicines, indigo, gold and jewels), Persia (silks) and China (rhubarb, tea, porcelain and medicinal herbs) could be bought and sold. Trade with Russia also grew significantly, with Bukharans exchanging cotton for leather, furs, cloth and metal items. Trade caravans to and from Russia typically numbered 4,000–5,000 camels carrying hundreds of tonnes of cotton – raw, spun and material. However, by the 1820s, the Khokandis of the Ferghana Valley were significant competitors to the Bukharans in trade with Russian Siberia.

The origins of the Khokand Khanate dated back to 1710, when the Min, an Uzbek nomadic tribe, moved into the Ferghana area from the north. They established their capital in the small settlement of Khokand, fortifying and expanding it. Boasting direct connections to both Tashkent and Samarkand, Khokand quickly became an important economic and cultural centre, remaining stable domestically while making useful political connections, such as formally accepting Qing overlordship. Here Bukharans brought raw cotton, English cheesecloth and plant materials for dyeing, and left with tea, porcelain and silk, and Russian iron and metal goods. Khokandis transported Russian goods to Kashgar and returned with Chinese products. Trade was given a boost between 1785 and 1792 when the Qing temporarily closed the market in Kyakhta on the northern border with Russia, and hence the Siberian Road, and the khanate was able to ship Chinese tea and rhubarb to Russian markets. A dispute with the Qing over customs duties then led to military confrontation and a Chinese boycott of trade – another significant blow to Silk Road trade – before a treaty was signed in 1832 that gave the Khokandis what they wanted.

For all this enduring context of thriving trade, during the latter half of the 19th century growing Western involvement in China, China's internal problems, Britain's expanded role in India and Russia's annexation of increasing swathes of Central Asia altered the connections between northern and southern Asia. Combined with the expansion of maritime trade in the Indian Ocean, this led to further erosion of Eurasian trade. As trade and traffic along the Silk Road declined, the economies of the settlements along its length suffered, in many cases catastrophically. Only the larger oasis towns and cities, and those with dependable water supplies, survived. The remainder were slowly depopulated and then abandoned. The swirling desert sands quickly engulfed the roads and tracks, the villages, towns and cities, the farmland and irrigation canals, until the greatest overland trade route in human history was all but obliterated.

The Tribute System

Use of the tribute system by the Chinese court dates back millennia, from before the unification of China under the Qin dynasty during the third century BCE. Principally serving to manage trade with, and pacify, China's neighbours, the system involved representatives from 'barbarian people' formally presenting gifts at the Chinese court in recognition of the advantages that an alliance with China would bring to their country. In return, they typically received lavish gifts – usually of a value greater than those they had offered.

The fortress of Khudayar Khan in Khokand was constructed in the 18th century. The state covered a region spanning modern Kyrgyzstan, eastern Uzbekistan, Tajikistan and southeastern Kazakhstan.

The ritualized interaction reinforced China's desired power dynamic between the two parties: the tributaries were submissive and reverent, acknowledging the emperor's supremacy, while the emperor was compassionate and condescending. Tributary missions were given imperial protection as they made their way to and from the capital and permission to trade in special officially supervised markets.

The illegal importation of opium by the British was halted during the Qing dynasty. Here, Commissioner Lin Zexu oversees the destruction of opium at Canton (Guangzhou) in 1839.

Over time, the countries and regions that sent tributes to China encompassed not only the bulk of Asia but locations further afield. A detailed list from the Ming dynasty in 1587 includes tributes from 38 countries of the Western Regions. Indeed, from the late Ming dynasty onwards, tributary trade made up the bulk of China's mercantile interactions with the world beyond its borders.

The system eventually collapsed towards the end of the 19th century, its demise brought about by the introduction of the treaty system after the Opium War of 1840. The last tribute mission was sent by Nepal in 1908.

— 6 —
REDISCOVERY

Over the centuries, many Silk Road stopovers – cities, oases, garrison towns, caravanserais – declined and even disappeared, due to climatic changes that caused water supplies to dry up or changes in the political and/or commercial landscape. By the end of the 19th century, much of the original infrastructure of the central Silk Road had been buried by the shifting sands of the Taklamakan Desert. Oasis dwellers shared tales of forgotten cities submerged under the dunes. Some of the ancient trade routes were still being used by itinerant merchants leading camel caravans, but the glory days of the old Silk Road were long since passed.

In fact, the term 'silk road' itself wasn't actually coined until 1877, when the German geographer and traveller Ferdinand von Richthofen (one of the founders of modern geography as an academic discipline) used the word '*Seidenstrasse*' (literally 'silk road') to describe the ancient trade routes across Central Asia in the first volume of his five-volume study *China*. According to von Richthofen, the account of Alexander von Humboldt's travels in 1829, *L'Asie Centrale*, had the greatest influence on his thinking about Asian geography, but it was the geography and world map of Marinus of Tyre – of which we know only indirectly through Ptolemy's *Geography* – that was central to his conception of a silk route through Central Asia from the Mediterranean to China.

However, while von Richthofen realized the central importance of silk in the east–west trade through Central Asia, and also the importance of the Eurasian steppe in the development of that trade, his conception of the Silk Road was limited, focusing almost exclusively on the relatively brief period when Rome and Han

*The German geographer Ferdinand von Richthofen (1833–1905) introduced the term 'silk road' (*Seidenstrasse) *in 1877. He was the uncle of the famous World War I flying ace Manfred von Richthofen, the 'Red Baron'.*

— TIMELINE —

1870 *Nikolai Przhevalsky's first expedition*

1876 *Przhevalsky's second expedition; Grigory Potanin's first expedition*

1877 *Term 'Silk Road' first coined by Ferdinand von Richthofen*

1879 *Potanin's second expedition; Regel's second expedition, Przhevalsky's third expedition*

1881 *Regel's third expedition*

1883 *Przhevalsky's fourth expedition*

1884 *Potanin's third expedition*

1892 *Potanin's fourth expedition*

1893 *Sven Hedin's first expedition*

1899 *Hedin's second expedition; Pyotr Kozlov's first expedition; Potanin's fifth expedition*

1900 *Library Cave discovered; Aurel Stein's first expedition*

1902 *First German Turfan expedition; first Japanese expedition*

1904 *Second German Turfan expedition*

1905 *Hedin's third expedition; third German Turfan expedition; Barrett-Huntington expedition*

1906 *Stein's second expedition; Paul Pelliot's expedition; Baron Carl Gustav Emil Mannerheim expedition*

1907 *Stein buys manuscripts from Library Cave; Pyotr Kozlov's second expedition*

1908 *Second Japanese expedition*

1909 *First Russian Turkestan expedition; Sergei Malov's first expedition; Arthur Sørensen's first expedition*

1910 *Third Japanese expedition*

1913 *Fourth German Turfan expedition; Stein's third expedition;*
Malov's second expedition

1914 *Second Russian Turkestan expedition*

1915 *Sørensen's second expedition*

1921 *Sørensen's third expedition*

1923 *Langdon Warner's first expedition*

1925 *Warner's second expedition*

1927 *Hedin's fourth expedition*

1930 *Stein's fourth expedition*

1931 *Chinese authorities close archaeological sites to foreigners*

China traded with each other along the overland routes; he believed that the routes fell into disuse with the fall of the Western Roman Empire and Han withdrawal from Central Asia. According to von Richthofen, as the Islamic trading world gained prominence, 'the concept of the transcontinental Silk Roads... lost its meaning'.

The new term took a while to catch on. In 1910, the scholar Albert Herrmann used it in the title of one of his books but then, in 1936, one of von Richthofen's students, the Swedish explorer Sven Hedin, published *The Silk Road*, which covers part of his final Central Asian expedition. Although Hedin barely uses the term in the book, as a popular account of the exploits of a famous explorer, it was influential in the term's uptake. Even so, it wasn't until the 1960s that it began to be used widely.

Sven Hedin
Born in Stockholm, Sweden, in 1865, Sven Anders Hedin was an explorer whose archaeological discoveries in Central

Asia sparked a period of intense Western interest in the region. Drawn to exploration from a young age, Hedin travelled in the Caucasus, Persia and Mesopotamia after finishing school. He later studied physical geography in Berlin under Ferdinand von Richthofen, the scholar who coined the term 'silk road'.

Over the course of four expeditions between 1893 and 1935, Hedin discovered the important sites of Dandan-Uiliq, Karadong and Loulan, mapped the Tarim River, pinpointed the sources of the Brahmaputra and Indus rivers, and solved the mystery of the shifting position of the dried-up salt lake of Lop Nor. Slight of frame and with poor eyesight, Hedin was, nevertheless, a strong and indefatigable explorer. He tended to travel with a small party, aided by a well-chosen coterie of local helpers. He was an accomplished linguist (fluent in seven languages), a skilled surveyor, an accomplished artist and a prolific writer; in addition to publishing some 65 books and numerous voluminous scientific reports, he wrote thousands of scholarly and political papers.

Hedin was made a Swedish noble in 1902, knighted by India in 1909 and received two of the Royal Geographical Society's coveted gold medals. He died in Stockholm in 1952.

Inspired by his mentor to explore Central Asia, Hedin arguably did more to bring the Silk Roads to the popular consciousness than anyone else. It was the reports from his early expeditions that brought news of the existence of a lost world in the deserts of Central Asia to Europe, sparking an intense archaeological 'gold rush', with numerous expeditions mounted by explorers from Russia, France, Finland, Japan, Denmark, Germany and Great Britain following in his wake.

By the time of Hedin's first expedition, in 1893, several Russian geographical expeditions had returned from Central Asia with tales of long-abandoned, sand-entombed settlements. Indeed, the results of these expeditions had fed into von Richthofen's thoughts on the Silk Road. But the first real evidence that a collection of lost cities lay hidden beneath the sands was gathered by an Indian clerk named Mohamed-i-Hameed. Sent by the lieutenant-governor of the Punjab on a secret surveying mission in the Taklamakan in 1863, Mohamed-i-Hameed learned that sandstorms occasionally exposed some of the old houses of the long-abandoned Tarim Basin oasis town of Khotan, once a provincial capital, now effectively wiped off the map. Two years later, a surveyor named William Johnson visited a buried city near Khotan and even managed to obtain an ancient brick of tea that had been salvaged from another ruin. In 1873, Sir Douglas Forsyth, a Punjab civil servant, found such tea bricks for sale in a market and was told that they had been dug up near Khotan. Two of his helpers managed to obtain some figurines, jewellery and coins that were also from a buried city.

The Russian expeditions – one in 1876–77 led by the celebrated explorer Colonel Nikolai Przhevalsky (also spelled Prejevalsky) and another in 1879 by the botanist Albert Regel – discovered a number of archaeological sites, including the ruins of a huge walled city that was eventually identified as the ancient Uighur capital of Karakhoja (Gaochang in modern Chinese, near Turfan). However, the expeditions were focused on broader geographical questions and they didn't spend time excavating the ruins they found.

By this time, local treasure-hunters were getting in on the act, particularly when they realized that foreigners would pay for their finds. In 1889, a party of treasure-hunters found a fifth-century manuscript in a ruined stupa near Kucha that eventually reached the Asiatic Society of Bengal in Calcutta (modern day Kolkata). The discovery and publication of the so-called Bower manuscript (named after Lieutenant Hamilton Bower, the Indian army intelligence officer who bought the document for Calcutta) is considered by

In 1879, the Russian botanist Albert Regel discovered the ruins of the ancient Uighur capital of Karakhoja deep in the Taklamakan Desert.

many to have instigated the serious archaeological investigation of Central Asia.

And so it fell to the young, bespectacled Swede Sven Hedin to uncover the hidden mysteries of the old Silk Road. During his first, four-year expedition, 29-year-old Hedin travelled via Russia to the Tarim Basin. Like the Russian teams, his interests lay more in conducting geographical and geological studies, but he undertook archaeological digs as well, in the hope that the results would provide evidence to support his ideas about how the basin's landscape had changed over time.

Having heard tales of lost, treasure-filled cities in the Taklamakan, Hedin resolved to find one for himself and duly set off from Kashgar on his first attempt to cross the desert on his 30th birthday – 17 February 1895 – a journey that very nearly claimed his life. Travelling with four local men, eight camels, two guard dogs, three sheep and 11 chickens, he got into trouble just over two weeks into the trek when he ran out of water. Six days later, Hedin, alone by this point, managed to reach the Khotan River. Two of his companions survived, along with one of the camels; the other two men were never seen again. In January the following year, before leaving Central Asia, Hedin explored archaeological sites around Khotan and discovered the important sites of Dandan-Uiliq and Karadong deep in the Taklamakan.

In 1899, he set out on his second expedition. After travelling through the Taklamakan by boat – perhaps a surprising form of transport for a desert, but he mapped the Yarkand and Tarim rivers as he went, as well as the dried-up salt lake of Lop Nor – in March 1900 he discovered the ruined Chinese garrison town of Loulan near Lop Nor, one of the most important crossroads on the main Silk Road route from Dunhuang to Korla. It was actually one of his workers who found the site, stumbling on the ruins after becoming disoriented during a sandstorm while recovering a spade.

A year later, Hedin explored Loulan in detail, excavating several houses, and uncovered a wealth of artefacts, including numerous Chinese manuscripts from the Western Jin dynasty that provided startlingly in-depth insights into everyday life. Hedin later suggested that the town had perished after a change in the course of the Tarim River caused Lop Nor to dry up. The expedition eventually resulted in almost 1,150 pages of maps.

Chinese Central Asia's incredible archaeological bounty was a result of the region's aridity: the dry desert air and encasing sand helped to preserve the detritus left behind when settlements were abandoned. Wooden tablets, silk tapestries, paper manuscripts, cave paintings and everyday objects such as goat-leather moccasins, woven rugs and string made from hemp (not to mention human bodies mummified by nature, discovered some decades later), which would have quickly rotted away in a more humid environment, survived in a remarkable state of preservation for thousands of years.

As information and antiquities continued to trickle out of the region, they piqued the interest of a Hungarian-born employee of the British Indian government by the name of Aurel Stein. Although very similar in age, Stein and Hedin differed in many ways. Hedin was an explorer first and foremost, while Stein was a talented Orientalist who explored for the sake of gaining access to sites that would help him to test his theories about the history of Central Asia – his particular interest was the influence of Indian culture on the area's ancient cities. Careful and meticulous in his approach, he liked to describe himself as an 'archaeological explorer'. Fortuitously, during a year's national service in the Hungarian army he had been trained in field-surveying techniques.

In January 1896, Sven Hedin uncovered the ancient site of Dandan-Uiliq, which required hard work to excavate as the sand soon filled in the areas that had already been unearthed.

Stein's first expedition took place in 1900–1 while the Chinese Boxer Rebellion was underway. Aged 37 when he set out from Srinagar in Kashmir, he travelled with four companions and a terrier named Dash. After waiting out the end of summer in Kashgar, the party headed to Khotan. (Learning from Hedin's experiences, Stein worked mostly during winter. Consequently he avoided the worst of the desert heat, but had to contend with temperatures that dropped as low as -10°C.) The route along the Tarim Basin's southern rim was at least partially chosen to follow that taken by the seventh-century Buddhist pilgrim Xuanzang, who had long been a hero of Stein's. By following in Xuanzang's footsteps, he hoped to identify some of the sacred sites the pilgrim mentioned in the book he wrote about his journey, *Great Tang Records on the Western Regions*.

After an 11-day trek into the Taklamakan, battling soft sand into which the feet of both men and camels sank, they reached Dandan-Uiliq. Stein had hired 30 men armed with traditional hoes to dig for him. It was difficult, tiring work; in places, they were digging down through almost 10 m (33 ft) of extremely uncooperative sand to get at the ruins beneath. (As Hedin wrote: 'As fast as you dig it out, it runs in again and fills up the hole.') But the rewards were substantial. During the first day of digging – an investigation of a temple already picked over by local treasure-hunters – the party made 150 different finds. Following three weeks of excavations, during which 14 buildings were investigated and the whole site surveyed, they excavated a few more sites.

Before heading for home, Stein took time to expose a fraud. A local treasure-hunter by the name of Islam Akhun had been selling manuscripts and books that he and a few associates had manufactured and artificially aged. The works had fooled several scholars in Europe, but Stein was suspicious, and when he confronted Akhun, the treasure-hunter eventually confessed to the deception.

Sir Marc Aurel Stein

Marc Aurel Stein was an archaeologist and geographer known for his explorations and archaeological discoveries in Central Asia. Born in 1862 in Budapest, Hungary, Stein

The Hungarian-British Aurel Stein (1862–1943) also made four expeditions to Central Asia, always accompanied by a dog. He had seven dogs in succession, all named Dash.

studied Oriental languages and archaeology at university before going on to work in academia in India.

After reading Sven Hedin's 1898 book *Through Asia*, Stein petitioned the British Indian government for support for an expedition to Central Asia. Between 1900 and 1930, he carried out four such expeditions, although the fourth was aborted after the Chinese authorities cancelled his visa. He returned from his second expedition with thousands of manuscripts from the recently discovered Library Cave near Dunhuang. His collecting activities, in particular the liberation of the Dunhuang manuscripts, made him a controversial figure; in China, he was dubbed a burglar and protests were staged.

Stein became a British citizen in 1904, received the Royal Geographical Society's Founder's Medal in 1909, and was knighted in 1912. He went on to become superintendent of the Indian Archaeological Survey and continued his studies of Alexander the Great's eastern campaigns, identifying the site of Alexander's storming of the Rock of Aornos. Stein died in Kabul, Afghanistan, in 1943, and was buried in Kabul's British Cemetery.

As news of the discoveries made by Stein during his first expedition spread through the antiquarian community in Europe, they attracted intense interest. Inevitably, others decided it was time to get in on the act. First out of the gates was a small group of Japanese Buddhist monks, who set off for Central Asia in August 1902, followed closely by a German expedition organized by staff from the Berlin Ethnological Museum. Led by the head of the museum's Indian section, Professor Albert Grünwedel, the expedition travelled to the oasis town of Turfan. Almost five months of excavations in the surrounding area unearthed 46 cases of material – success enough to justify a return visit.

The second German expedition, again centred on Turfan, spent almost four months excavating at Karakhoja, where they uncovered evidence of the town's past as a centre of the Manichaean religion. The expedition then travelled to the Buddhist cave complex of Bezeklik. Taken aback by the amazingly well-preserved paintings they found there, they set about removing them from the walls for transport back to Berlin. A third German Turfan expedition, which began in 1905, continued the plunder. At the Buddhist cave complex near the town of Kizil, the Germans removed many more paintings. In all, some 620 murals and fragments were eventually returned to Berlin.

While the Germans were at work at Kizil, Aurel Stein was setting out on his second expedition. It was during this foray, in 1906–8, that he was to make his most celebrated, and most controversial, discovery. But first, travelling in a large party that contained 50 labourers and 25 camels, as well as 30 donkeys loaded with blocks of ice for drinking water, he excavated several sites on his way to Loulan, the oasis garrison town that Hedin had discovered seven years earlier. Stein and his team spent 11 days working at Loulan, uncovering a wealth of ancient military records as well as a collection of tablets bearing writing in Kharoshthi, an ancient script used in northwest India. The presence of these tablets suggested to Stein that as well as acting as a garrison for Chinese soldiers, at some point Loulan had also served as an outpost of an ancient Indian empire. The expedition also stopped in Miran, where Stein discovered a series of murals containing some distinctively Western elements, such as cherubs – further evidence of the extensive cultural exchanges that had taken place along the Silk Road.

Stein's next stop was Dunhuang, a town that he had been keen to visit since 1902, when he had heard of its splendours from Lajos Lóczy, a Hungarian geographer who had visited the nearby

Albert Grünwedel (1856–1935) led the first German expedition to Turfan and uncovered many wall paintings, including this Buddhist image of the 'Merciful Turtle King' from the Kizil caves, dating from the fifth or sixth century.

Mogao Caves in 1879 during a Hungarian expedition to Central Asia. On the way there, Stein was transfixed by a line of ancient watchtowers in the desert that he correctly identified as the remains of the westerly extension of the Great Wall. He planned to return to investigate further, but not long after arriving in Dunhuang, he was told of an enormous cache of manuscripts discovered in a walled-up room in the Mogao cave complex. He was forced to wait to see the hoard, however, as their discoverer, the self-appointed caretaker of the caves, a Daoist monk by the name of Wang Yuanlu (or Abbot Wang, as he's often known), was away attempting to raise funds for his 'restoration' of the caves. In the meantime, Stein investigated the watchtowers, locating the legendary Jade Gate – the final frontier for merchants heading west from China.

When Abbot Wang finally returned, Stein and his assistant, Chiang Ssu-yeh, set about the delicate task of convincing him to sell them some of the manuscripts. The breakthrough came when Stein mentioned his devotion to Xuanzang, and the fact that he was retracing the journey of the ancient pilgrim. Abbot Wang was a fellow follower, and his reticence towards the foreigner instantly vanished. Stein was able to enter what became known as the Library Cave and, eventually, to leave Dunhuang with a collection of about 10,000 documents packed in 24 cases. Among them was the world's oldest-known printed book, a ninth-century copy of the *Diamond Sutra*, one of the Buddha's sermons.

The Diamond Sutra *(868BCE) is the earliest surviving dated printed book. This shows the highly detailed frontispiece, drawn in ink on paper.*

Differing points of view

When called upon to justify their plunder of Central Asia, many of the Western explorers described it as 'rescue'. In his book *Buried Treasures of Chinese Turkestan*, Albert van Le Coq, who led some of the German expeditions, says that his 'borrowings' were necessary because of the turbulent nature of Chinese Turkestan at the time. There's some merit to this defence. Over the years, numerous murals were defaced and otherwise damaged by local Muslims, often because of aniconism, the Islamic proscription against images of sentient beings; local farmers dismantled ruined buildings, using the earth on their fields and the beams for fuel, and planted crops around them, causing further damage through irrigation; earthquakes caused caves to collapse; local treasure-hunters destroyed statues in pursuit of gold and silver.

Unsurprisingly, the Chinese see things differently, talking of 'colonial rapacity' and comparing the 'theft' of material to the taking of the Elgin Marbles. In the Chinese 'league table of perfidy', Aurel Stein sits at the top, followed closely by Paul Pelliot and Sven Hedin. Since the end of foreign expeditions in Central Asia, the Chinese government has periodically used the perceived indignities as a way of stirring up nationalist sentiment.

Stein wasn't the only Westerner to partake of the cave's bounty. In 1908, the French Sinologist Paul Pelliot shipped another large part of the collection back to Europe, amounting to some several thousand manuscripts, as well as silk banners, paintings and rare wood sculptures. Pelliot was accompanied on the expedition by a photographer named Charles Nouette, who took thousands of photographs of the caves, which have proven to be invaluable for the study of the murals they contained, many of which were later damaged. Japanese, Russian and Danish explorers also acquired collections of the manuscripts. By the time that the Chinese scholar and antiquarian Luo Zhenyu arranged for the remaining manuscripts to be moved to Beijing in 1910, only about a fifth of the original collection remained.

A professor of Chinese at l'Ecole Française d'Extréme Orient in Hanoi, Vietnam, Pelliot was an accomplished linguist, speaking 13 languages. Crucially, one of those languages was Chinese, which was a great asset when obtaining supplies for his 1906 expedition, and would prove even more helpful later. Pelliot's expedition visited Kucha, where he found documents in the lost language of Kuchean, and Ürümqi, where he heard about the Dunhuang manuscripts. Examining a sample document, he immediately recognized its archaeological importance and set off for Dunhuang, arriving in

Paul Pelliot (1878–1945) poses with military and civil mandarins in 1908 in Hami, one of the northern Taklamakan oasis towns.

March 1908, three months after Stein. Gaining access to the Library Cave, he spent the next three weeks poring over the vast hoard of manuscripts, often reading by candlelight long into the night (he claimed to have read up to 1,000 documents a day). Here, again, his linguistic skills were invaluable. Unlike Stein, who didn't speak Chinese, Pelliot could read and assess many of the documents, selecting those with the greatest value. Abbott Wang, who was interested in continuing the refurbishment of his monastery, agreed to sell them to Pelliot.

'Sorry for drinking so much'

Among the tens of thousands of documents recovered from the Library Cave was an unusual 'sample letter'. Written in Chinese, it was designed for inebriated guests to pass to their offended hosts by way of apology for their behaviour:

Yesterday, having drunk too much, I was so intoxicated as to pass all bounds; but none of the rude and coarse language I used was uttered in a conscious state. The next morning, after hearing others speak on the subject, I realized what had happened, whereupon I was overwhelmed with confusion and ready to sink into the ground with shame....

This was then followed by a sample reply for the host:

Yesterday, Sir, while in your cups, you so far overstepped the observances of polite society as to forfeit the name of gentleman and made me wish to have nothing more to do with you. But since you now express your shame and regret for what has occurred, I would suggest that we meet again for a friendly talk....

The numerous expeditions to Central Asia at this time took place in a politically charged atmosphere. Britain and Russia were playing out the 'Great Game', tussling for control over the region:

the Russians were concerned about the commercial and military inroads that Britain was making in Central Asia, while Russia's own Asian empire-building had Britain nervous about losing India. Consequently, a few of the expeditions were effectively fronts for spying operations.

The most infamous was that of Baron Carl Gustaf Emil Mannerheim, a colonel in the Russian army. (He was actually Finnish, but at that time Finland was part of tsarist Russia.) Mannerheim was sent to Central Asia by the Russian General Staff to study the political and economic situation and gather military intelligence. Posing as an ethnographic collector, he joined Paul Pelliot's expedition after meeting him on a train in Samarkand. However, the two didn't get along, and parted ways after crossing the Altai Mountains and entering China. Mannerheim went on to visit Khotan, Turfan (where he purchased numerous manuscripts and other antiquities), Kashgar, Ürümqi and Dunhuang, before following the Great Wall through the Hexi Corridor and eventually returning to Russia in 1909.

The Library Cave

On 25 June 1900, an itinerant Daoist monk by the name of Wang Yuanlu, who had appointed himself caretaker of the Mogao caves near Dunhuang, was smoking a cigarette in Cave 16. He noticed that the smoke was slowly wafting away from the entrance and, curious, he knocked down part of the cave's back wall, revealing a hidden chamber. Inside, he found more than 14 cubic metres (500 ft^3) of bundled manuscripts piled more than 3 m (10 ft) high. Wang reported his find to the local authorities and tried to convince government officials of the value of his discovery but they were low on funds and preoccupied with the Boxer Rebellion, and the cache remained in its cave.

Seven years later, news of the find reached Aurel Stein, who was then on his second expedition to Central Asia. Stein rushed to Dunhuang but was forced to wait two months

The Daoist monk Wang Yuanlu, a caretaker at the Dunhuang caves, discovered the so-called Library Cave, but the government did not look into his find, as they were more concerned with the ongoing Boxer Rebellion.

before being able to speak to Wang. He eventually convinced the monk to sell him some 10,000 documents and painted scrolls. Later French, Japanese, Russian and Danish explorers also left Dunhuang with collections of the manuscripts.

Originally built during the Tang dynasty, between 851 and 867, as a memorial chapel to an eminent monk, the Library Cave was sealed up sometime around the middle of the 11th century and a mural was painted over the wall. It's unclear why the relics were hidden, but the most popular theory is that the monks were hoping to protect them from an imminent invasion.

The cave contained the largest collection of cultural relics ever discovered on the Silk Road, including more than 40,000 manuscripts dating from the fifth to the early 11th centuries. About 90 per cent were religious in nature, relating mostly to Buddhism, but also to Daoism, Manichaeism, Zoroastrianism and Nestorian Christianity.

The remainder is a fascinating mixture of official and private correspondence, literature, phrase books, calendars, social and economic documents such as sale contracts, loan and pawn-shop documents and accounting ledgers, and reference works covering such subjects as medicine, mathematics, weaving, history and winemaking. Most are written in Chinese, but there are also manuscripts in Khotanese, Sanskrit, Sogdian, Tangut, Tibetan, Old Uighur, Kuchean, Hebrew and Old Turkic.

In 1994, the International Dunhuang Project began to restore and digitize the manuscripts recovered from the Library Cave and many of them are now available to view online.

The next few years saw a flurry of expeditions, with parties from Denmark, Japan, Germany, Russia and the USA making their way to the Tarim Basin. The fourth German Turfan expedition set off in 1913 but was curtailed by the beginning of World War I. Aurel Stein undertook his third expedition the same year, returning with more manuscripts from Dunhuang and a collection of early textiles from the cemetery of Astana, as well as more than 100 cases of murals from Bezeklik.

The US expedition, led by 42-year-old art historian and archaeologist Langdon Warner of Harvard University's Fogg Art Museum, arrived in Central Asia in 1923. By now, the activities of previous expeditions were starting to have an effect on the availability of artefacts. At Karakhoto, the visitors found the site picked clean by Stein and a Russian team. They moved on to Dunhuang, where they were horrified to discover that many of the ancient cave paintings had been vandalized by White Russian soldiers: having fled over the border after the outbreak of the Russian Revolution, 400 soldiers had been imprisoned in the caves for six months and had taken their boredom out on the murals. Warner had come armed with a special glue and he set about using it to peel some of the paintings from the cave walls. Over the course of five days, he removed 12 paintings, which he took back to Harvard.

This was to be one of the last Central Asian expeditions to return to the West with a significant collection of artefacts. Indeed, the window of opportunity for foreign explorers proved to be relatively narrow, lasting from the Russian and Hungarian expeditions in the late 1800s to the early 1930s, after which, belatedly, the Chinese government closed the country's archaeological sites off to the 'foreign devils' whom it accused of plundering its antiquities. Matters came to a head in 1925, when the second US expedition, again led by Warner, arrived in Dunhuang, to be met by groups of openly hostile locals and suffer harassment from officials. After only three days at the Mogao Caves they were forced to abandon the expedition. Sven Hedin was only able to carry out his fourth and

The Mogao Caves, also known as the Thousand Buddha Grottoes, line a low cliff-face outside Dunhuang. They contain a wealth of intricate Buddhist cave paintings and several large statues.

final expedition (1927–35) by collaborating with Chinese scholars, who kept all of the material it uncovered. Stein attempted to mount a final expedition in 1930, but it was curtailed by the authorities and his finds were confiscated. In 1931, China's National Commission for the Preservation of Antiquities declared that the export of archaeological objects could only be justified if 'there is no one in the country of their origin sufficiently competent or interested in studying or safe-keeping them. Otherwise, it is no longer scientific archaeology but commercial vandalism.'

Although foreigners were no longer welcome, Chinese archaeological campaigns continued their work. Among the first Chinese scholars to make his name in archaeology was Huang Wenbi, who took part in the 1926–35 Sino-Swedish expedition to the Gobi Desert and Mongolia, led by Sven Hedin and Xu Xusheng. Huang went on to lead further archaeological expeditions to the region from the 1950s, unearthing numerous important artefacts and discovering several new sites, but was killed in 1966 during the Cultural Revolution. From the 1980s onwards, Chinese archaeologists have made extensive excavations in the Xinjiang region, yielding remarkable finds along the old Silk Road.

TOURISM ALONG THE SILK ROAD

Just as news of the amazing archaeological discoveries in Central Asia was reaching Europe, the region was being closed off to foreigners. Following the Russian Revolution of 1917, the '-stans' – Kazakhstan, Kyrgyzstan, Turkmenistan, Uzbekistan and Tajikistan – were annexed by the new Union of Soviet Socialist Republics, while in China the end of the imperial era and the formation of the new Republic of China ushered in a long period of nationalism and isolationism characterized by a distrust of foreigners, particularly from the West.

During the Soviet period, foreign tourism to Central Asia was strictly controlled, with a limited number of cities open to visitors and heavy penalties for any foreigners who went 'off piste'. The lifting of the Iron Curtain during the early 1990s following the collapse of the USSR opened up Central Asia to the West for the first time since the Revolution.

The situation in China was broadly similar. Travel was greatly restricted before and during the 27-year reign of Mao Zedong. Following his death in 1976, the social and market reforms under Deng Xiaoping and his successors saw tourism become increasingly important to the Chinese economy as restrictions were dropped. These changes led to rapid growth in international visitor arrivals, which rose from 1.8 million in 1978 to 128 million in 2014.

Across the Middle Eastern sections of the Silk Road, tourism has been equally sporadic. Countries such as Iran have largely been relatively closed to outsiders, while Iraq and Afghanistan, in particular, having been accessible if uncomfortable in the days of 1960s hippie trails, have been off-limits during times of war – and some of their most fascinating sites destroyed by extremists.

At present, tourism in Central Asia is still beset with problems – notably a lack of tourist infrastructure, stifling levels of bureaucracy, internal conflict and endemic corruption. The UN World Trade Organization (WTO) is working to promote tourism along the Silk Road, focusing primarily on improving collaboration among the countries along the ancient trade routes. In particular, it hopes to create a bespoke visa regime that would allow tourists to travel freely around the region.

Visitors who manage to navigate the logistical hurdles are rewarded with the architectural wonders of magnificent Silk Road cities such as Samarkand and Bukhara, as well as intriguing cultural and archaeological sites such as the Mogao and Kizil caves in western China, and Merv and Nisa in Turkmenistan. Although independent travel in Central Asia remains relatively difficult, organized tours with private companies – some focusing solely on the Silk Road – are increasing.

Uzbekistan, which boasts a relatively well-developed tourism infrastructure and some of the most impressive architecture in the region, is currently the most popular destination. The country hosts more than 4,000 historical and cultural monuments, among them the crown jewels of Islamic architecture; 140 sites have been inscribed on the World Heritage list. Visitor numbers to Uzbekistan increased tenfold between 2005 and 2013, from about 200,000 to almost two million.

The Silk Road is a very attractive tourism 'brand'. It's widely recognized and instantly evokes a rich and fascinating cultural history tinged with mystery and exoticism. It also benefits from the cachet of novelty – the regions through which it passes are still relatively untouched by modern tourism. In 2014, the Central Asia region hosted about 11 million visitors (the UK welcomed about 34 million the same year). The numbers for Central Asia are rising rapidly, however, and the WTO is working to build a sustainable and resilient tourism sector along the Silk Road in order to avoid

Some aspects of Silk Road life have been adapted to attract tourists. Here, visitors explore the sand dunes of the Gobi Desert by camel.

the damage that unplanned mass tourism can cause. Many sites along the route are extremely fragile and will quickly be damaged if tourist numbers aren't controlled in some way.

China has been committing significant resources to tourism projects in Xinjiang Uighur Autonomous Region in the country's northwest, where most of its Silk Road cultural heritage sites are located. Home to several ethnic groups, including Uighur, Kazakh, Tajik, Kyrgyz, Mongol and Russian, the region has suffered from unrest in recent decades, and the Chinese government is keen to improve its image and bring tourists back. A thriving tourism industry would also provide employment in the restive region, where rural poverty is endemic.

WORLD HERITAGE LISTING

The United Nations Educational, Scientific and Cultural Organization (UNESCO) has since 1972 compiled a list of more than a thousand worldwide sites of cultural or natural significance for humankind. It encourages their protection and appreciation, and regularly adds further locations.

In 2014 the Chang'an–Tian Shan Corridor was designated a World Heritage site. This listing covers a 5,000-km (3,000-mile) section of the Silk Road stretching across three countries, from the ancient Chinese capitals of Chang'an and Luoyang through Kyrgyzstan and into the Zhetysu region in Kazakhstan. It includes more than 30 nominated archaeological sites and other places of interest that, collectively, cover an area of 42,668 ha (105,434 acres), with a 190,000-ha (470,000-acre) buffer zone. They include capital cities, palace complexes of empires and kingdoms, trading settlements, Buddhist cave temples, ancient paths, post houses,

The Fengxiangsi Cave in the Longmen Grottoes in the ancient Chinese capital of Luoyang is just one of the impressive UNESCO World Heritage sites found along the Silk Road.

passes, beacon towers, sections of the Great Wall of China, fortifications, tombs and religious buildings.

The degree to which these sites are being protected or made available to travellers varies considerably. Due to the fragility of many sites, growing tourism may be damaging. There are also concerns about the impact of urban, rural and infrastructural development, or changes in agricultural practices. Indeed, all of the 11 archaeological sites in the Zhetysu region have been backfilled and covered for protection and to control deterioration.

It's hoped that the Chang'an–Tian Shan Corridor listing will be followed by other Silk Road inscriptions. The Indian portion of the Silk Road is on the tentative site list and the Maritime Silk Road is also being considered. Work is underway to submit an application for a second Silk Road World Heritage Corridor: the Ferghana–Syr Darya Corridor would take in parts of Kazakhstan, Kyrgyzstan, Tajikistan and Uzbekistan. The South Asian region, covering countries such as Bhutan, India and Nepal, is preparing Silk Road-related nomination dossiers too.

— 7 —
TRADE ALONG
THE SILK ROAD

Silk Road trade was, by and large, caravan trade. Just as today lorries, rail cars, container ships and cargo planes carry goods from city to city and country to country, so strings of camels, horses, oxen, donkeys and, occasionally, yaks were the transport fleet of a complex ancient logistics industry. However, the popular image of large caravans loaded down with trade goods travelling over vast distances is probably erroneous. The archaeological evidence suggests that much of the private trade along the Silk Road was carried out by what were essentially small-scale pedlars whose 'territories' were relatively small, perhaps covering three or four towns over distances of a few hundred kilometres.

As they made their way along, the merchants would stop at caravanserais to rest and replenish supplies, and perhaps do some small-scale trading, before stopping at their ultimate destination, where they would sell their cargo and then take on a new supply of goods to carry back the way they had come. Hence goods often changed hands several times during their journey from one end of the Silk Road to the other. An individual item's value increased each time it changed hands, so goods were often extremely expensive when they reached their final destination. The merchants also incurred numerous incidental costs as they travelled, such as the bribes and commissions they had to pay to the various middlemen and officials they dealt with during their journeys, which further pushed up prices.

Whenever possible, transit traders would finish a trip (and then begin a new one) in one of the many Silk Road hubs, such as

Samarkand, Bukhara or Dunhuang, where several trade routes came together. This east–west trade was supplemented by a north–south trade, whereby nomads from the north brought livestock and other products to Silk Road settlements to trade for items they couldn't produce themselves.

However, a significant proportion of the 'trade' along the Silk Road actually took the form of government 'payments' to garrisoned troops and other public servants. It was this regular influx of large quantities of silk and other commodities that sustained the economies of many of the towns and smaller settlements along the route, rather than the smaller volume of private trade. For example, in 745, a garrison near Dunhuang received two shipments of silk from the Tang government totalling some 15,000 bolts. As this government-provided silk was 'spent' within the settlements – to buy food and other necessities – it provided local merchant communities with large quantities of the material, which they could then trade for Central Asian and other foreign products. Another source of silk and other luxuries for oasis traders was the tribute trade exacted by the nomads – usually in exchange for horses – which would eventually trickle down to merchants in the oases. During the Tang dynasty, up to 90,000 bolts of silk a year were flowing from China into the Western Regions.

Goods were paid for using a mixture of different exchange media, including coins, silk, grain, rugs, bartered goods and, eventually, paper money. Coins were made from a range of metals: gold (although many of these were fake), silver, copper, lead and bronze. Because coins were often in short supply – because the metal from which they were made was often in short supply – Chinese government regulations stated that bolts of silk should be used for larger purchases, such as slaves and livestock, while coins were to be used for cheaper items.

The traders and merchants who plied the Silk Road had a diversity of origins. At various times, Sogdians, Chinese, Indians, Arabs, Turks, Uighurs, Bukharans, Greeks, Jews and Italians were

Detail from a colourful mural painting entitled The Ambassadors' Painting *(c.650), a rare example of Sogdian art found in Afrasiyab, an ancient site in northern Samarkand.*

active in Central Asian trade. Of these, it was the Sogdians who were the most significant players, dominating exchanges with China and India, and setting up business communities in central China, the Tarim Basin and elsewhere along the different trade routes.

This well-preserved terracotta statuette of a Silk Road camel driver dates from the Northern Wei dynasty (386–534). Camels were well suited to the challenging conditions of the route and could cover a distance of 1,609 km (1,000 miles) in eight weeks.

As trade along the Silk Road grew, so too did the mercantile infrastructure within the larger settlements. Commercial companies, often family enterprises, developed to cover the organization of goods transportation. There were brokers to arrange contracts, banking houses to offer credit, money-changers and caravanserais for accommodation. Cities also provided warehousing, as well as dedicated market areas and merchants' rows. In larger settlements, these might be divided up according to the types of merchandise they offered: goldsmiths in one, hat sellers in another, a market for mulberry leaves and another for livestock. Although foreign trade items were sold in these markets, the bulk was usually locally produced.

Most caravans were small-scale – often only four or five people and about ten animals – but in some cases camel caravans could include hundreds or even thousands of heavily-laden animals carrying dozens of tonnes of merchandise and tended by tens, possibly hundreds, of merchants, servants and porters. An entry in the dynastic history of the Zhou mentions a caravan bound for Wuwei, in modern Gansu province, that consisted of 240 non-Chinese merchants transporting 10,000 bolts of multi-coloured silk.

Local people, including nomads, often acted as caravan guides (caravanbashis), leading merchants on the often difficult-to-follow routes through the desert. Sometimes nomadic herders would accompany a caravan with their livestock, providing cattle for food and transportation as required. Caravans also often hired translators and, when banditry became a problem, they would take on guards. During such periods, merchants often gathered together for safety in numbers.

In camel caravans, the beasts were roped together, head to tail, in groups of five to ten, walking at about the same pace as a man. At the end of a journey, the camels would be left to rest and recover, while the merchants gathered a new team for the return journey. Merchants might hire or buy camels, which usually cost 14 bolts of silk. A merchant who hired a camel was responsible for its return in good condition.

And the Silk Road could be a dangerous place. Starvation, thirst, heat stroke, hypothermia, venomous snakes, spiders and scorpions, disease and bandits were all potential threats. Ferocious sandstorms could, at the least, cause animals to run away, travellers to become disoriented or a path to disappear; at worst, they could bury an entire caravan. Flash floods could wash travellers away, particularly during spring and summer as the previous winter's snowpack melted. Travel through the mountain ranges that intersected the trade routes brought its own dangers, including slipping from the rough, narrow tracks, avalanches and rock falls, and hypothermia; the passage across the Pamirs is known as the Trail of Bones in recognition of the numerous people who lost their lives negotiating it.

Travellers along the part of the Silk Road that passed through China were kept under close government scrutiny. All were required to apply for an official document – in effect a Silk Road passport –

The route across the Pamir Mountains from Osh in Kyrgyzstan to Mazar-e-Sharif in Afghanistan is known as the Trail of Bones due to the many dangers facing those who follow it.

when they arrived at the border. These travel passes, typically made from strips of poplar wood, listed the members of the party: first men, then women and livestock. As travellers passed from region to region, they were required to stop at guard stations, where local officials checked that all of the people and animals in the travelling party rightfully 'belonged' to the primary traveller. In the case of the animals, this would usually involve producing a market certificate to prove that they were purchased legitimately. At each station, the caravans' passes were scrutinized and then replaced with new ones. The documents were dated, verified by a witness and carried instructions for the officials reading them: 'Let them pass. If their party is more than what is listed here, do not allow them to pass.' Travellers were prohibited from diverging from their itineraries without official permission.

Because camels and other beasts of burden couldn't carry extremely heavy or bulky goods over the mountains and across the deserts, raw materials such as lumber were rarely transported along the overland Silk Road. Instead, it was used primarily to transport smaller luxury items with high value-to-weight ratios, such as silk, precious stones, incense and spices. Among the goods brought to China via the Silk Road were dates, saffron powder and pistachios from Persia; frankincense, aloes and myrrh from Somalia; glassware, gold and other precious metals, cut precious stones and amber from Rome; spices from Southeast Asia; and ivory, cotton and sandalwood from India. Caravans travelling in the opposite direction carried, among other things, bolts of silk, jade carvings, paper, lacquerware, steel, leather products and porcelain and other ceramics.

During the medieval era, slaves – often soldiers and civilians captured in battle or raids – were an important commodity, and some cities along the Silk Road, such as Khiva and Bukhara, featured dedicated slave bazaars, although most of the trade was carried out on a more informal basis in caravanserais and smaller settlements. According to one estimate, during the Tang era 80 per cent of caravans passing through the Turfan region dealt with slaves, who accounted for almost 40 per cent of all travellers. Many were bought by, and toiled under, the nomads. By the 18th century, slavery was being progressively outlawed, and the trade began to decline.

Paper Money

Paper currency of a sort was first used during the Tang dynasty, in around 800. Known as 'flying cash' because it had a habit of blowing away, it took the form of certificates issued by the government as an alternative to shipping heavy copper coins to distant areas. The certificates could be converted into coins at the capital and, as they were transferable, merchants exchanged them as though they were currency.

The Song dynasty saw the first use of true paper currency, issued by private merchants and banks in Sichuan province. It was circulated widely and readily accepted for payment. However, in 1023 it was withdrawn and replaced by official banknotes printed by the government. Inflation ensued because the government didn't hold enough coins to cover the value of the paper currency it issued.

During the 13th century, the Mongols forcibly reintroduced paper money within China, leaving the Chinese more silver coinage to use for trade with Central Asia. However, once again, excessive printing flooded the market, and the paper money depreciated rapidly.

An attempt by Gaykhatu, a late-13th-century Ilkhanate ruler in Persia, to impose paper money there was even more disastrous. Merchants refused to accept the banknotes, and riots broke out. After economic activity largely ground to a halt, Gaykhatu was forced to withdraw the paper currency. He was assassinated soon afterwards.

ROUTES

The Silk Road was a long way from what we think of as a road today. Unpaved and generally unmarked, the different routes that made up the Silk Road were rarely even discernible, hence the need to hire guides. Not only did geography restrict the routes that could be taken, forcing travellers over high mountain passes and across deserts, but the routes themselves often shifted on both small and large scales according to changing conditions – heavy snowfall, a flood, a dune moved onto the track by a sandstorm, the imposition of a new regional levy or perhaps the outbreak of war.

Leaving the Chinese capital, Chang'an, travellers would proceed westward through the Hexi Corridor, between the Gobi Desert and the Qilian Mountains. After passing through the Jade Gate, effectively the end of China proper, most would head to Dunhuang, where a decision had to be made: circle around the Taklamakan Desert by the northern or the southern route? Or even risk the central route through the desert itself? This was one of the most arduous sections and was typically navigated during winter, when temperatures were less brutal. Otherwise, caravans travelled at night to avoid the worst of the heat. They would also break up the journey, stopping at the settlements and caravanserais that ringed the Taklamakan for days, weeks or longer. And a few would avoid the Taklamakan altogether by taking a path north of the Tian Shan to Ferghana and Sogdiana.

The Taklamakan routes converged in the city of Kashgar. From there most entered the so-called Pamir Knot, where the great mountain ranges of the Tian Shan, Karakoram, Kunlun, Hindu Kush and Pamirs come together (although a few groups branched out, for instance south via the Karakoram to India). This section brought new challenges, as some of the passes reach altitudes in excess of 4,000 m (13,000 ft).

Once on the other side of this formidable barrier, travellers could head south towards India or continue west to the legendary cities of

Samarkand, Bukhara and Merv, and on via an array of routes to Persia and the Middle East before finally reaching the Mediterranean. Thus 'northern' and 'southern' Silk Roads may refer either to the two main routes around the Taklamakan or to the various options west of the Pamirs between Central Asia and the Mediterranean.

CARAVANSERAIS

As trade along the Silk Roads developed, so too did the infrastructure required to house and feed the merchants. Central to this were large guesthouses designed to accommodate travelling merchants and their caravans. Although they bore different names in different countries, they are now widely known as caravanserais, a term derived from two Persian words: *kārvān* or *karwan* (caravan or group of travellers) and *saray* or *sara* (place, house or simply enclosed building).

Travel along many sections of the route was dangerous, so wherever possible, caravanserais were positioned within a day's journey of each other – about 30–40 km (19–25 miles) apart in areas where the route was well maintained, a distance that could be covered, on foot, in about eight to ten hours. This meant that merchants (and, importantly, their precious cargo) could avoid spending the night exposed to the dangers of the road. In some cases, particularly in areas close to territorial frontiers, caravanserai walls were heavily fortified, the buildings playing a dual role as hotel and military outpost.

While they provided travellers with a secure place to spend the night and prepare for the next day's journey, caravanserais were also important meeting places for trade and communication with locals and other travellers, and hence were of great economic, social and cultural significance: far more than simply inns, they acted additionally as hubs of intercultural dialogue – crucibles for cross-fertilization of cultures. Merchants would have shared their stories and experiences and, ultimately, cultures, ideas and beliefs. Many of the cities that contained caravanserais, such as Samarkand, Qazvin, Bursa, Aleppo and Acre, would eventually become intellectual and cultural centres, while caravanserais located in more isolated areas became local centres of civilization.

With so many different cultures and races living along the routes, merchants had to be able to speak at least a smattering of several different languages, and the caravanserais provided an ideal venue for learning those languages, along with the rules of etiquette. Travellers were also often able to fulfil their religious duties at the caravanserais, many of which were furnished with mosques.

The buildings frequently resembled fortresses: typically square or rectangular, with strong exterior walls built from local materials – burnt bricks, clay and stones – and a large gate to allow for the entry of bulky goods and animals. Inside, a large open-air courtyard was surrounded by a series of small rooms for accommodation, barns for housing animals and storerooms for trade goods. Rooms were basic, lacking windows or other ventilation, but often having a small

Cities such as Aleppo became thriving centres of trade and culture, their caravanserais providing opportunities for the exchange of both goods and stories.

veranda to protect them against the sun and rain. In some, bigger corner rooms were available for travelling government officials. Many caravanserais provided guests with somewhere to bathe, and some would even have a doctor on site. In many, a bazaar would be set up in the courtyard to enable trade to take place both among the travelling merchants and with local inhabitants.

From around the tenth century, construction of caravanserais intensified, as the various trade routes through Central Asia became more lucrative and the volume of business increased. The resulting network of caravanserais stretched from China to the Indian subcontinent, Iran, the Caucasus, Turkey, and as far as North Africa, Russia and Eastern Europe, numbering in the thousands. Many still stand today.

A typical caravanserai is a large square or rectangular roadside structure where merchants and animals could rest overnight while travelling. This example is in Fars province in modern-day Iran.

The Sogdians
Although they were responsible for the construction of such renowned cities as Samarkand and Bukhara, and were key players in the commerce of the Silk Road, we know relatively

little about the Iranian-speaking peoples known as the Sogdians.

Sogdiana was effectively a collection of city-states rather than a unified nation, primarily centred in what is now northern Tajikistan and southern Uzbekistan, especially around Samarkand. This is more or less the area that was

A relief frieze from Persepolis, Iran, shows Sogdian delegates with rams during the Achaemenid period (c.515BCE).

also at times known as Transoxiana. The Sogdians lived in fertile valleys surrounded by deserts, the most important of which was the Zeravshan Valley.

However, they also established extensive colonies in what is now western China, and there were Sogdian outposts in cities and markets along the length of the Silk Road. At the height of the Silk Road, in particular between the fifth and eighth centuries, the Sogdians were one of the primary go-betweens in trade exchanges in Central Asia and China, and the main caravan merchants of the Silk Road.

So wide-reaching was their influence that, during the seventh century, the Sogdian language was effectively the lingua franca of Central Asia. Around the tenth century, Sogdian culture effectively vanished as their language was subsumed into the Persian-speaking world.

SILK

According to Chinese tradition, silk was first developed sometime around 2700BCE, although there is evidence that sericulture, the process of making silk, may date to as far back as 5000BCE. From its early beginnings, silk was considered to be an extremely high-value product and was reserved for use exclusively by the imperial court. Eventually, however, it was adopted widely through Chinese society.

This 12th-century Chinese painting (after Zhang Xuan, 713–755) shows Tang-dynasty court ladies preparing newly woven silk.

The Chinese are thought to have begun trading silk by the first millennium BCE. Remnants of what is probably Chinese silk from 1070BCE have been discovered in Egypt, and archaeologists have found Chinese silk dating from about 500BCE in Afghanistan. By the Han dynasty, when the overland Silk Road 'officially' opened, silk was one of China's main exports.

Sericulture and the origin of silk

Silk is produced by a number of different invertebrates, but one, a species of silkworm found in China (*Bombyx mori*), is uniquely suited to the production of high-quality silk fabric. The caterpillar of a now-flightless moth, the silkworm feeds on mulberry leaves, eating continuously and eventually growing to about 10,000 times its original weight. The worms that hatch from 6 g ($^1/_5$ oz) of eggs will eat 200 kg (440 lb) of leaves before they pupate, at which point they will produce about 1 kg (2.2 lb) of raw silk.

When mature, the caterpillar begins to produce a glandular secretion that dries into a threadlike filament, which it uses to form a cocoon over the course of three or four days. The filament, typically about 300–1,000 m (1,000–3,300 ft) long, is extremely strong and can be unravelled. First, the cocoon is boiled to kill the pupa inside and dissolve the gum resin or sericin that holds the cocoon together. It's then soaked in warm water and unwound. The dried filaments are combined to form a silk thread and wound on to a reel. Silk threads are then spun together, often with other yarn added. This thread can be dyed and woven into material on looms. It takes about 2,000–3,000 cocoons to produce enough silk to make a dress.

Silk is an extremely versatile fabric. It keeps the wearer cool in summer and warm in winter; it's very absorbent, so it holds dyes more efficiently than cotton, wool or linen; it has an attractive 'shimmering' quality and drapes over a body particularly well; and it's fire and rot resistant.

It's said that the Romans first saw high-quality silk in 53 BCE, when the Parthians unfurled their banners before the Battle of Carrhae. Rome took to silk as an exotic luxury and it quickly became extremely popular with the empire's elite. Over time, however, the Roman leadership became deeply conflicted about it. While they admired its qualities, they deplored the economic imbalance that it exemplified – such was the appetite for silk that the balance of trade was usually heavily stacked in China's favour. In short, large quantities of Roman silver were being used to buy large quantities of Chinese silk.

Rome's leaders were also concerned about the decadence and excess that they believed that silk represented. With supplies limited, many merchants unravelled and rewove their fabric into thinner, virtually transparent garments in order to stretch out their stocks. 'I can see clothes of silk – if materials that do not hide the body, nor even one's decency, can be called clothes,' wrote Seneca the Younger, an imperial advisor. 'Wretched flocks of maids labour so that the adulteress may be visible through her thin dress, so that her husband has no more acquaintance than any outsider or foreigner with his wife's body.' In response, the Roman Senate issued several edicts banning the wearing of silk clothing. For example, according to the Roman historian Tacitus, in the year 14 CE the Senate made it illegal for men to wear silk, resolving that 'Oriental [Eastern] silks should no longer degrade the male sex'. Perhaps inevitably, these bans had little lasting effect.

Silk remained popular in the Mediterranean region even after the fall of the Roman Empire in 476. Its successor, the Byzantine Empire, carried on the Roman infatuation with silk, particularly in the church and among the ruling classes. The silk worn and used by these elites was typically dyed purple, using a special dye made from a mucous secretion from predatory sea snails found in the eastern Mediterranean.

Silk wasn't just used to make clothing; it was also turned into fishing lines and used for making paper and the strings of musical instruments. It even became a general medium of exchange: Chinese farmers paid their taxes in locally-produced silk, and civil servants received their salaries in silk. It was widely used as a diplomatic gift too. By the sixth century, silk thread (known as floss) had become more popular as a commodity than silk material. In Persia and around the Mediterranean, the floss was woven into designs and styles to suit local tastes.

The Imperial Secret
The techniques used for the production of silk were a fiercely guarded secret within China for some 3,000 years. According to imperial decree, anyone who revealed the secret to a foreigner faced execution. These efforts were largely successful; even in the early years of the first century CE, people in the West believed that silk grew on trees. However, China didn't have a complete monopoly on silk production. Chinese immigrants brought sericulture to Korea in around 200BCE, it was established in India by 140CE and it was widely known in Japan by about the third century CE.

The secret of sericulture finally reached the West during the sixth century CE. Legend has it that during a visit to China in 552, a pair of Nestorian (Assyrian Christian) monks concealed some silkworms and mulberry seeds in their bamboo walking sticks and smuggled them back to Constantinople, the capital of the Byzantine Empire. There,

Detail from a Song-dynasty painting (ink and colour on silk) shows women placing silkworms on trays of mulberry leaves. The caterpillars eat the leaves, then spin their silken cocoons.

the monks' smuggled material and knowledge formed the basis for a local silk industry that provided religious vestments and aristocratic dress across Europe.

By the Tang dynasty, silk was also being produced by the Persians and various peoples across Central Asia. However, Chinese silk continued to be in high demand due to its exceptional quality.

— 8 —
THE TRADE
IN IDEAS

While the Silk Road has traditionally been thought of as a collection of trade routes, it could be argued that its central importance to the history of Eurasia, and indeed the world, was actually related to the flow of ideas rather than goods. Technological innovations, religious beliefs, languages, medical knowledge, cuisines, architectural styles, even town-planning techniques all made their way east and west across Eurasia and over the sea via the Silk Roads.

Sometimes the spread of ideas was a side-effect of war. Refugees fleeing conflict were regularly to be found moving along the Silk Road in search of a safe haven, bringing ideas and cultures with them. The spread of Islam across Central Asia was largely brought about by the subjugation of peoples through imperial conquest. And both Timur and the Mongols moved artisans and intellectuals from subjugated territories to their imperial capitals. Papermaking reached the Islamic world when Chinese soldiers with knowledge of the technology were captured in an eighth-century battle; Chinese weaving techniques are said to have crossed over at the same time.

However, trade was the most influential mode of cultural and technological transmission. Western traders brought wheeled transportation and different forms of metallurgy to China; in return, China gave the world the magnetic compass, the mechanical clock, the umbrella, the crossbow, the kite and the wheelbarrow. Islamic merchants, active across the networks, created new financial institutions and instruments, including international banks and joint-stock companies, and invented double-entry bookkeeping.

The Invention of Paper

For centuries, the Chinese used bamboo, wooden strips or silk to write on. None of these were particularly convenient – silk was expensive and wood and bamboo were bulky and heavy. The 'official' date for the invention of paper is 105CE – roughly when trade along the overland Silk Road was beginning to blossom. That year, Tsai Lun, director of the imperial workshops at Luoyang, produced a report to the

This engraving depicts early Chinese papermaking using a pulp made from crushing bamboo stalks.

emperor on the process of papermaking, describing how he broke up the bark of a mulberry tree into fibres and pounded them into a sheet. However, archaeological investigations suggest that the actual invention of papermaking took place in southeastern China about 200 years earlier, largely using hemp fibres.

Paper was initially used primarily as wrapping for medicines and tea, but its use for writing soon followed. It quickly spread throughout China and East Asia, although uptake was limited as it was relatively expensive. The Chinese were loath to share the secret of paper manufacture and even attempted to create a monopoly by stamping out other Oriental production centres. Then, in 751, the Arab Abbasid Caliphate defeated Tang Chinese forces at the Battle of Talas. Among the captured Chinese soldiers were some who knew how to make paper and, before long, a small industry developed in Samarkand. The methods soon made their way to Baghdad, where the world's first paper mills were established towards the end of the eighth century. The Arabs, too, jealously guarded the secret, and it didn't reach Europe until around the 12th century.

During the sixth century CE, the Chinese invented block printing, a development that was quickly embraced by Buddhism, which attributed religious merit to the act of duplicating sacred texts. This innovation was followed by the creation of moveable type during the 11th century, also in China. The inventions of paper and different forms of printing were extremely influential in the spread of literature and literacy, as books became both more convenient to use and cheaper.

An Explosive Idea

Among the technological innovations that moved along the Silk Road is one that can be genuinely called history-changing. Gunpowder was invented by Chinese alchemists seeking immortality towards the end of the Tang dynasty, although references to similar substances go back as far as Han times. It took centuries for gunpowder to evolve from a 'special effect' used in acrobat and puppet shows to fireworks to a sophisticated weapon of warfare. By the 12th century, the Chinese were using gunpowder in simple cannons and guns. Around this time, gunpowder was introduced to the Arab world, before moving on to Greece and the rest of Europe, altering the geopolitical balance across Eurasia and ushering in a new era of warfare.

Textiles were so central to Silk Road trade that it's unsurprising that technology related to textile production spread along it. The first looms were probably developed in Egypt, but underwent significant development in China, with each new iteration spreading out to weavers in Mesopotamia and beyond. The earliest evidence of the pattern loom, for example, which revolutionized silk production, was found in a tomb in Chengdu, southwest China, that dates from the second century BCE.

The dissemination of irrigation technology – including the noria waterwheel, invented in Roman Syria in about 300, based on earlier Egyptian waterwheels – enabled farmers to cultivate arid land in Central Asia. It's doubtful that the Silk Road could have functioned as it did without the settlements that were sustained by this technology. Other examples of farming technology that spread along the Silk Road include the seed drill, planting crops in rows and the iron plough, all of which were invented in China.

Paddle-driven noria waterwheels, like these examples on the banks of the Orontes River in Hama, Syria, allowed water to be lifted into aqueducts for irrigation.

LANGUAGE

Over the history of the Silk Roads – both overland and maritime – hundreds of different languages have been spoken in the territories that they connected. Broadly speaking, the languages of the overland Silk Road fell into four main groups: Indo-European, Sino-Tibetan, Turkic and Mongolic. And just as those languages changed from region to region, so too did they change from time to time, mostly as a result of territorial expansion and contraction – that is, it wasn't just languages that changed but entire peoples. One of the side-effects of this was that a bewildering array of languages were spoken across Central Asia; to date, records of 28 different languages have been discovered in the Tarim Basin alone, some of which were unique to the region. The most common were Khotanese, Tocharian, Sogdian and Chinese.

177

For travelling merchants, the problem of mutual incomprehension had a number of solutions. They could learn to speak at least a smattering of several languages, hire translators or perhaps carry a phrasebook. Several such phrasebooks were among the documents found in the Library Cave in Dunhuang, one of which was clearly compiled for Tibetan merchants travelling to China. Along with the names of goods, including food, clothes, tools and weapons, it contains a series of phrases related to buying and selling, such as 'last price' and 'thanks for letting me look', and words and phrases that would be useful for people looking for food and a bed for the night in a foreign town.

However, a simpler solution was for traders to adopt a lingua franca – a common language in wide use across a region, much like English and Spanish are today. Over the years of the Silk Road, a number of lingua francas were employed. In its heyday, the language of the Sogdians was a lingua franca for trade across Eurasia. During later periods, when Islam became the dominant religion along the Silk Road, the lingua franca became Persian. Following the Tibetan Empire's conquest of parts of eastern Central Asia during the eighth and ninth centuries, Tibetan also acted as a lingua franca for some time. And since the 19th century, when Russia began to colonize Central Asia and the Caucasus, Russian has been the lingua franca over much of the region.

With so many people speaking different languages travelling so much and interacting so regularly, conditions were perfect for the exchange of linguistic elements; that is, the languages themselves were in constant flux. Today, it's possible to identify numerous so-called loan words – words from one language that are incorporated into another without translation – in the languages spoken in Eurasia.

The predominant language teachers and translators of the Silk Road were Buddhist monks, who worked tirelessly to translate sacred Buddhist texts from India into the local language and to convey Buddhist teachings to potential converts. Among the most successful translators was Kumarajiva, a monk from the oasis town of Kucha. Working in Chang'an as the head of China's translation bureau at the start of the fifth century, he and other translators developed a system whereby certain Chinese characters and their sounds were used to represent each syllable of a foreign word – analogous to the use of phonics in English teaching today. The practice, which is still in use, caused Chinese itself to change, adding an estimated 35,000 words to the language.

MUSIC

Music forms an integral part of virtually all human cultures, so it's unsurprising that there was a vibrant exchange of musical styles and instruments along the Silk Road. As physical objects, instruments are the easier of the two to follow over time, and numerous examples exist of musical instruments that have spread along the Silk Road, including cymbals, which were introduced to China from India, the harp, which originated in Mesopotamia, and Chinese gongs, which made their way to Europe. The ancestors of the oboe and flute are also thought to have originated in either China or Central Asia and spread along the Silk Road to Europe, while there are the suggestions that steppe nomads may have been the first to use a bow to make music on a stringed instrument.

Religion played a key role in the transmission of musical culture along the Silk Road, as did the bazaars, caravanserais, taverns and teahouses in which travellers mingled. Sufi Muslims, for whom music, singing, chanting and sacred dance were elements of prayer, were highly mobile, wandering the Islamic world and spreading the word to audiences that gathered to hear them. Similarly, travelling Buddhist monks transferred different forms of sacred chant from one part of Eurasia to another. They were also probably responsible for the spread of the *sheng*, or Chinese reed-pipe mouth organ. Thought to have originated in southern China and incorporated into Chinese orchestral music by the fifth century BCE, the *sheng* became associated with Buddhist liturgical music in China,

This 13th-century artwork from the illustrated manuscript Hadith Bayad wa Riyad *depicts music being played on the oud, an Arabic stringed instrument.*

spreading into Korea and Japan and to the oasis Buddhist temples of Central Asia.

As musicians travelled the Silk Road, so too did musical styles and productions. Often originating in India, musical dramas – depictions of the lives of the gods, popular legends or just everyday life – would evolve as they travelled, absorbing local elements to make them more relevant to, and hence popular with, their audiences. And just as we see today, musical styles changed over time, coming in and out of favour. During the Tang dynasty, the music of the oasis town of Kucha became especially popular in China; the town's musicians and dancers, the talk of the Tarim Basin, were even celebrated by Chinese poets. The music of the Tang court was based on the tuning of the Kuchean lute and many among the nobility were proficient on the Kuchean drum. Emperor Xuanzong housed about 30,000 musicians and dancers within the imperial palace, many of whom performed in Kuchean style. The style was also transmitted from China to Japan, where its influence can still be heard today in *gagaku* or Japanese court music.

MEDICINE

Medical knowledge, along with the medicines themselves, also travelled in both directions along the Silk Road. Buddhist monks copied and translated into numerous languages the works of famous Chinese and Arab medical authors, as well as anonymous Tibetan collections of cures for contagious illnesses. The manuscripts recovered from the Library Cave in Dunhuang include part of a book called *Master Ling Yang's Secret Remedies*, a text entitled 'The Ten Fatal Maladies' and another that contains a cure for baldness: 'Rub in horse-mane oil regularly; the hair then begins to grow spontaneously.' The Tang era saw a great flowering of medical study, with Chinese scholars and physicians absorbing medical information from the Islamic world and India. Arabic pharmacies opened in China.

At around the same time, the House of Wisdom in Baghdad was on its way to becoming the Arab world's great centre of learning. Established by the Abbasid caliphs Harun al-Rashid and his son al-Ma'mun during the eighth to ninth centuries, it attracted scholars from far and wide, many of them dedicated to translating Greek, Persian and Sanskrit texts into Arabic. In particular, there was a great thirst for medical knowledge, and the scholars pored over the works of Hippocrates, Galen and Dioscorides, compiling and summarizing what they found to create a consistent medical system. Before long, Islamic medicine became the most sophisticated in the world.

Since Baghdad was also home to the world's first paper mills, the Arabs were able to set about publishing the results of their studies.

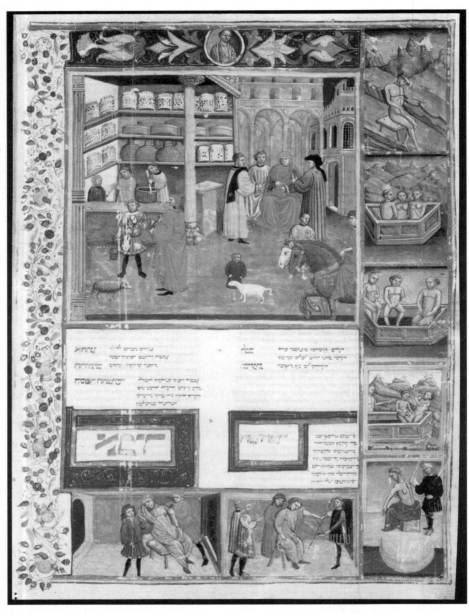

This page from The Canon of Medicine *by the Persian scholar Ibn Sina (Avicenna) is written on vellum. The five-volume work, completed in 1025, was a standard textbook in Europe for six centuries.*

Among the most influential works was the *Canon of Medicine*, which helped physicians to diagnose diseases such as cancer. Written by the doctor and philosopher Ibn Sina (also known as Avicenna) during the early 11th century, it went on to become one of the most famous medical works of all time, in use in Europe until the 17th century.

CUISINES

The ubiquity of certain dishes along the Silk Road – noodles, dumplings and kebabs, for example – is testament to the ancient sharing of culinary information among Eurasian civilizations. When new ingredients arrived – novel spices, fruits, vegetables and grains – they were incorporated into a region's cuisine and chefs came up with ways to cook them, often using knowledge passed on by the traders and envoys who brought them.

As with the passage of other ideas, sometimes the dissemination of culinary information was the result of imperial conquest. In northern India, the rise of the Islamic Mughal Empire during the 16th century introduced a Persian-based cuisine, while in the southwest there are dishes strongly influenced by the Portuguese, who ruled a colony in Goa for 400 years.

Although the origins of the noodle are hotly debated, it's clear that noodles spread along the overland Silk Road, and today they are part of the cuisine of almost all its countries. In 2002, archaeologists discovered a 4,000-year-old bowl of noodles made from broomcorn and foxtail millet in China – the oldest known example of the dish. However, wheat-based noodles only became a significant part of Chinese cuisine after the Han dynasty, when the technology for building mills for large-scale flour grinding arrived via the newly-opened Silk Road. By the end of the dynasty, Chinese chefs had developed the techniques, still in use today, for swinging dough into individual strands. The wheat grown in China wasn't suitable for making the noodles we know as pasta and it was probably the Arabs who introduced noodles, together with the hard durum wheat necessary for making them, to Italy during the ninth century.

Another globally ubiquitous dish, the dumpling, may well have had multiple origins. It's thought that Chinese dumplings date back to the Han dynasty, while the first known recipe comes from *Apicius*, a Roman recipe collection probably compiled during the first century CE. The Turkic peoples embraced the dish and some researchers have suggested that it spread across Eurasia with the Mongols.

RELIGION

In the centuries leading up to the opening of the Silk Road, the peoples of Eurasia followed numerous different religions. At the western end, many worshipped the gods and goddesses of the Graeco-Roman or Egyptian pantheons, while others followed Mithraism, a faith originally of Persian origin. Jewish merchants and other settlers had spread Judaism beyond the ancient kingdoms of Israel and Judaea. In China, ancestor worship was common among the ruling class, while peasants often had animistic or shamanic beliefs, and all these intermingled with the principles of Taoism.

Over time, new religions developed, many of which spread out along the developing trade routes. Pilgrims and missionaries from

This 15th-century artwork depicts traders unloading spices from their ships.

a variety of faiths regularly journeyed along the Silk Roads, often accompanying trade caravans for protection. Travelling merchants were also responsible for the spread of religion; the Sogdians in particular were instrumental in the dissemination of all the major Silk Road faiths – Zoroastrianism, Manichaeism, Buddhism, Christianity and Islam – across Central Asia. And caravanserais acted as hubs for the sharing of ideas such as religion, with many containing mosques and shrines so that travellers could carry out their religious duties while far from home.

As they spread, religions often morphed to better suit the needs of the new cultures they encountered. Alexander the Great's Hellenistic legacy in Central Asia led to a mixing of Classical Greek and Eastern philosophies, creating syncretisms such as Graeco-Buddhism. When Buddhism reached China, it had to accommodate ancestor worship and the tenets of Confucianism, while Chinese Christianity had to incorporate Taoist and Buddhist terminology in order to make sense in its new context.

The spread of religion along the Silk Road wasn't always a peaceful process. The Muslim conquest of most of Central Asia was a major factor in the religion's dominance in the region. Muslim armies, intent on plundering the riches of subjugated lands, often targeted wealthy temples and shrines. In 1193, Muslim forces led by the Turkish leader Bakhtiyar Khilji destroyed the international Buddhist university at Nalanda (near modern Patna in Bihar state, northern India), effectively spelling the end of Buddhism in its birthplace.

ZOROASTRIANISM

One of the world's oldest monotheistic religions, Zoroastrianism was founded by the prophetic reformer Zoroaster (also known as Zarathustra) during the tenth century BCE (or possibly earlier) in what is now Iran. It became the dominant pre-Islamic religious tradition of the Iranian peoples and for 1,000 years it was one of the world's most powerful religions.

Zoroastrianism is a dualistic faith, based around the struggle between good and evil, both cosmically (God and the Devil, Heaven and Hell) and personally (righteous or evil). Zoroastrians believe in a single compassionate god, Ahura Mazda ('Wise Lord'), who created the universe and resides in Heaven. Ahura Mazda has an adversary, Angra Mainyu ('Destructive Spirit'), the originator of all that is evil, who dwells in Hell. As in Christian tradition, when a person dies they go to Heaven or Hell, depending on their deeds. The dualism at the heart of Zoroastrianism is thought to have been influential in the formulation of Jewish theology and, by extension, Christianity.

Although fire isn't worshipped as a deity, it's an important element in Zoroastrianism, representing an agent of purification and a symbol of God's light or wisdom. Zoroastrians worship communally in a fire temple or *agiary*.

After spreading across Persia, Zoroastrianism made its way into Central and East Asia along the trade routes that would become the Silk Road, most likely spread by the Sogdians. It's thought to have reached China as early as the sixth century BCE. In around 600BCE, it became the official religion of Persia, a position it would hold until around 650CE.

By the time the Achaemenid Persian Empire was founded in 549BCE, Zoroastrianism was well established. Its kings were pious Zoroastrians, but also tolerant of other religions. When Alexander the Great conquered Persia a century later, his troops persecuted Zoroastrians: priests were killed, religious texts were destroyed and Zoroastrianism was largely replaced by Hellenistic beliefs. The Seleucids, Parthians and Sassanians who ruled Persia after Alexander's death were more tolerant, and the Zoroastrian church became both more powerful and more wealthy. Under the Sassanians, the church and state became less tolerant of religions other than Zoroastrianism, and it was made a capital crime for a Zoroastrian to convert to another religion.

The invasion of Persia in the seventh century by Islamic Arabs saw Zoroastrians persecuted once again. Although they were allowed

The prayer hall of a Zoroastrian Fire Temple in Kerman, Iran. Holy Fire, or Atar, burns in the vase in the middle.

to continue to practise their religion, they were put under great pressure to convert to Islam. When the Abbasids overthrew the Umayyads in 750, the climate for non-Muslims became markedly harsher and many Zoroastrians were forced to either convert or migrate. Later invasions by the Turks and the Mongols brought further persecution.

Zoroastrianism is still practised in isolated areas of Iran and in parts of India, where it's also called Parseeism because its adherents are mostly descendants of Iranian immigrants known as Parsees. There are probably fewer than 190,000 followers worldwide.

BUDDHISM

Originating in India sometime between the sixth and fourth centuries BCE, Buddhism is largely based on original teachings attributed to the religious thinker known as the Buddha. Its central message is that earthly life is an endless cycle of birth, suffering, death and rebirth. Followers are taught that the cycle can be broken through Buddhist faith and ritual practice, the exact nature of which depends on the school of Buddhism followed.

Buddhism was the first large-scale missionary religion and the first to take advantage of the mobility offered by the Silk Road. Expanding out from the religion's homeland in northeastern India, Buddhist missionaries and merchants built temples, shrines and monasteries along the trade routes. In return for a donation, passing travellers could spend the night – or longer – in many of these structures, offering their priests and monks the opportunity to preach, which helped the faith to spread rapidly. This was aided by the wide appeal of Buddhism's message, whose universalism enabled it to cross cultural boundaries with ease.

As with other Silk Road religions, trade played a central role in Buddhism's spread and survival. Buddhist monks and nuns often accompanied trade caravans. Because they were required to give up all their worldly possessions, they depended on the lay community

The 27 m (100 ft) statue of the Maitreya Buddha standing alongside the Yellow River, near modern Lanzhou at the east end of the Hexi Corridor, is evidence of the arrival of Buddhism in China.

to supply necessities. Buddhist monasteries sustained themselves through material donations; in return, donors received religious merit, which could be shared with others, and perhaps religious instruction. The earliest donors and some of the most important patrons were caravan merchants and wealthy bankers. This arrangement supported the production of much of the art along the Silk Road. Donations that helped to finance the building of shrines, stupas and statues, or the painting of scenes from the Buddha's life in caves and other sites, generated special merit by providing opportunities for worship.

Buddhist demand for the 'seven treasures' – gold, silver, lapis lazuli, crystal (or coral), agate, red pearl and carnelian – which represented the seven powers of faith, perseverance, sense of shame, avoidance of wrongdoing, mindfulness, concentration and wisdom, also helped to stimulate trade. High in value but low in volume, these materials were ideal commodities for long-distance trade and the ritual values associated with Buddhism would have augmented their economic worth.

Faxian

During the early fifth century, Faxian, a 60-plus-year-old Chinese Buddhist monk, walked from China to India in the hope of acquiring Buddhist sacred texts. Along the way, he visited numerous Buddhist sites in what are now Pakistan, India, Nepal, Bangladesh, Sri Lanka and China. After ten years studying in India, he returned via the Maritime Silk Road but was blown off course twice and ended up spending five months in what is now Indonesia. In total, his journey took 15 years.

Afterwards, he wrote up his journey in a travelogue, *A Record of Buddhist Kingdoms*, which contains accounts of early Buddhism and the geography and history of the Silk Road nations through which he passed. He devoted the rest of his life to translating from Sanskrit to Chinese the many Buddhist texts he had brought back from India.

'In the desert were numerous evil spirits and scorching winds, causing death to anyone who would meet them. Above there were no birds, while on the ground there were no animals. One looked as far as one could in all directions for a path to cross, but there was none to choose. Only the dried bones of the dead served as indications.'

Faxian's description of crossing a Central Asian desert

The religion arrived in China around the middle of the first century CE and spread rapidly, aided by conversion of the ruling elites and a mixture of official and private support for the building of temples and monasteries. With the establishment of a base in Luoyang, China's capital at the time, Buddhist monasteries soon began to appear in the Silk Road oasis settlements around the Tarim Basin. In addition to preaching to passing travellers, monks in these monasteries were mostly concerned with translating sacred Buddhist texts from the original Sanskrit into the local vernacular. From the fourth century, Chinese pilgrims began to make the long journey back to Buddhism's birthplace in India in order to consult the original Buddhist scriptures.

By the fifth century, Buddhism was the dominant religion in China, a position it held until the mid-ninth century, when the Taoist Emperor Wuzong, who believed that Buddhism was a drain on the Chinese economy due to its tax-free status, issued an imperial edict forcing Buddhist nuns and monks to give their wealth to the state or return to lay life. Persecution increased over the following years, with confiscation and destruction of Buddhist temples and shrines and the removal of more than a quarter of a million monks and nuns from the monasteries. Although Buddhism remained important, it was more as a private than an officially sponsored religion.

The rise of Islam in Central Asia in around the seventh century effectively brought an end to the transmission of Buddhism along the Silk Road. Today, it's the world's fourth-largest religion, with more than 520 million followers, who live primarily on the eastern edges of the Silk Road, in Southeast Asia, China, Japan and Korea.

Xuanzang
Famed for his remarkable pilgrimage to India and his translations of the Buddhist scriptures with which he returned, the Buddhist monk Xuanzang was born into a family of scholars in 602 in what is now China's Henan province. After a classical Confucian education, he became

interested in Buddhism through an older brother and was ordained as a monk in 622.

Having identified discrepancies and gaps in the Chinese version of the Buddhist canon, he resolved to travel to India and find the missing documents. However, he was unable to obtain a travel permit so in 629 he slipped out of Chang'an, made his way along the Hexi Corridor and followed the northern route of the Silk Road around the Taklamakan Desert. Once in India, he visited all the sacred sites connected with the life of the Buddha, but spent most of his time at the Nalanda monastery, studying Sanskrit and Buddhist philosophy. In 643 he began his return journey, taking with him 657 Buddhist scriptures packed in 520 cases.

On arrival back in Chang'an two years later he was offered a ministerial post by the emperor but chose instead to devote himself to translating the scriptures he had brought from India. Although he only managed to translate a small portion of them, these included some of the most important works. He also founded a new school of Buddhism and wrote *Records of the Western Regions of the Great Tang Dynasty*, a record of the countries through which he passed on his pilgrimage.

Xuanzang (602–664) was a Chinese Buddhist monk who famously made a 17-year overland journey along the Silk Road. This portrait shows him on his way to India.

CHRISTIANITY

Based on the life and teachings of the prophet Jesus, who is believed to have lived from around 0CE to 32CE, Christianity is an Abrahamic monotheistic religion. Claiming to be the son of God – the benevolent creator of the world – Jesus' main teaching was that if people obeyed his rules for good living, they would spend eternity in Heaven rather than Hell. His death by crucifixion is said to have paid for the sins of the world.

During the first century CE, Christianity moved out of its homeland in what is now Israel and Palestine via existing Jewish communities and a group of proselytizing apostles. Around the middle of the third century, the religion's easterly spread was aided by the relocation of Greek- and Syriac-speaking Christians as a result of the Persians' successful invasion of eastern Roman territory. By the end of the fourth century, Christianity was the official state church of the Roman Empire.

In the fifth century, the Christian church underwent a schism over religious doctrine, splitting into western and eastern factions. The Church of the East, largely based in Persia, identified with the position held by the Patriarch of Constantinople, a Syrian bishop named Nestorius. Hence, Christians living along the Silk Road are often referred to as Nestorians. However, followers of the Church of the East weren't the only Christians to be found on the Silk Road – there were also Armenians, Georgians, Jacobites and others.

As the church spread east from Persia, it reached Sogdiana. Many Sogdians converted to Christianity and, as with other religions, they played an important role in its transmission along the Silk Road. Sogdian merchants were often multilingual and served as capable translators of Nestorian texts. By 650, there were archbishoprics in the Sogdian capital, Samarkand, and farther east in Kashgar.

Christianity is thought to have reached China in around 600, by which time there were Nestorian churches in cities along the length of the Silk Road. In 635, a group of Nestorians led by the Syrian missionary Alopen arrived in China, an event commemorated in a stele (standing stone tablet), dated 781, in Chang'an. The early Tang rulers, who promoted religious diversity, welcomed the Nestorians. The Emperor Taizong allowed Alopen to establish a monastery in Chang'an and asked him to translate the Christian scriptures into Chinese. Imperial favour helped the church to flourish, but in 845 Emperor Wuzong, a Taoist, decreed that all foreign religions were banned in China, sending the church into decline; by the tenth century, the number of Chinese Nestorians had dwindled to almost nothing. Elsewhere along the Silk Road, the rise of Islam during the seventh century curtailed the growth of Christianity, but the two religions were generally able to coexist.

Like the Silk Road itself, Christianity enjoyed a resurgence in China under the Mongols, who were highly tolerant of most religions. Many nomads had been converted by Nestorian missionaries – often Sogdians – who had been proselytizing to the steppe nomads from about the seventh century; indeed, several Mongol tribes were Christian. However, suppression returned under the Ming dynasty. The following centuries saw several waves of Christian (mostly Catholic) missionaries arrive in China amid alternating climates of acceptance and repression by various rulers. Today, Christianity is the world's largest religion, with more than 2.4 billion followers or roughly a third of the global population.

MANICHAEISM

Established by the Persian prophet Mani during the third century CE, Manichaeism incorporated elements of the other faiths of its time, including Zoroastrianism, Christianity, Hinduism and Buddhism. It focused on the struggle between good and evil, light and darkness, and offered salvation to those who were deeply immersed in its teachings. From the start, the church undertook vigorous missionary activity and, by adjusting to local cultural conditions, it was quickly able to spread along the Silk Road, eventually reaching as far west as Europe and as far east as China. In common with many other cultural exchanges at the time, Sogdian merchants played a central role in transmitting the faith to both the Chinese and the steppe nomads.

Passing through Egypt, Manichaeism reached Rome early in the fourth century, and churches were established in southern Gaul and Spain. But by the end of the fifth century it had been effectively wiped out in Western Europe after sustained attacks from both the Christian church and the Roman state.

When Tang forces reopened the Silk Road caravan routes during the seventh century, Manichaeism spread east, becoming established in China towards the end of the century. However, in 732, after imperial Buddhist officials came into conflict with it, the Tang emperor issued an edict prohibiting Manichaeism from being taught to native Chinese, although foreigners were still permitted to practise.

Not long afterwards, Manichaeism became the state religion of the Central Asian Uighur Khaganate after its ruler helped Tang forces suppress a rebellion in the Chinese city of Luoyang, during which he came in contact with resident Sogdian Manichaeans. It remained so until the khaganate was overthrown in 840. China placed a prohibition on the religion three years later, but in both regions it continued to be practised until the 13th or 14th centuries.

ISLAM

An Abrahamic, monotheistic religion, Islam was shaped by its prophet, Muhammad. Born in around 570 in Mecca (now in Saudi Arabia), Muhammad was a prosperous merchant who, at the age of 40, received a series of revelations from Allah (God) that were collected in Islam's sacred book, the Koran, which Muslims consider to be God's word. In essence, Islam's teachings are: belief in one merciful God, creator and sustainer of the world; the necessity of faith, compassion, morality and accountability in human behaviour; and the recognition that God has sent prophets and revelations to other societies.

Despite persecution by the authorities, Muhammad built a significant following during his lifetime, first by preaching and then

Mani, the prophet of Manichaeism, is portrayed in the centre of this 16th-century miniature from Uzbekistan. He is shown presenting King Bahram Gur with a painting.

by creating a larger community through political and military means. By the time of his death in 632, he had effectively united the Arab tribes. The question of succession led to a period of disruption and infighting, but the Muslim leadership eventually formed a series of caliphates that set about expanding Islam's reach through conquest. In this they were extremely successful and Islam underwent what was probably the most rapid and widespread dissemination of a religion in human history. Over time, it largely displaced most of the other faiths along the Silk Road, to the point where it's now the dominant religion in most of the countries through which the old Silk Road passed.

Although the initial spread of Muslim rule to neighbouring regions took place via conquest, religious conversion of the subjugated people tended to be peaceful, thanks to a Koranic injunction to spread the faith by example rather than coercion. It was brought about primarily through the work of Muslim scholars, missionaries (in particular the Sufis), traders, rulers and devout believers. However, sometimes Islamic governments made life difficult for non-believers, by measures such as higher taxation and laws restricting ownership of slaves, leading ultimately to their conversion. In many cases, non-Muslims were barred from government positions, which was also a strong motivation to convert. This was particularly true of those who had previously held privileged economic, social and political positions: becoming Muslim allowed them to rejoin the ruling group.

By the mid-eighth century, Muslims controlled the western half of the Silk Road, and trade began to play an increasingly significant role in the spread of Islam. Islam also played a significant role in the success of Muslim traders. Merchants held a favoured position in the Islamic world and, through their dominance of the overland and maritime trade networks, they could work together at the expense of non-believers. Muslim officials and Islamic laws both favoured Muslim traders. Many Muslims financed their pilgrimage to Mecca by carrying small amounts of merchandise to sell along the way.

Between the mid-eighth and the mid-13th centuries, Muslim scholars made numerous advances in science, engineering, technology, philosophy and the arts. Here, Turkish and Middle Eastern astronomers are depicted studying latitude in an observatory in Constantinople.

As they travelled, Muslim traders acted as proselytizers for their religion. This was particularly true in Southeast Asia and Africa, as mosques were established in Arabic trading communities in port cities around the Indian Ocean. Along the overland Silk Road, mosques were often set up in caravanserais. In China, Muslim merchants formed permanent enclaves. The settlers were permitted to take Chinese wives, but the women were prohibited from accompanying their husbands if they returned home. Under Islamic law, the children of a Muslim father must be raised as Muslims; consequently, Muslim Chinese minorities formed in many of China's trading cities, where they are still evident. Today, Islam boasts more than 1.8 billion followers or roughly a quarter of the global population; Muslims make up a majority of the population in 50 countries.

— 9 —
THE ECOLOGICAL SILK ROAD

The Silk Road was a conduit for the movement of myriad animals, plants and diseases. From the Neolithic onwards, exchanges among farming communities and nomadic pastoralists saw newly domesticated species spread east and west along what would become the Silk Roads. As trade grew, these exchanges gathered pace, eventually shaping the patterns of Eurasian – and, to a significant extent, African, thanks to the Maritime Silk Road – agriculture that we see today. Movement along the Silk Roads also encouraged the spread of disease, which was to have a profound effect on the rise and fall of empires in Central Asia and beyond.

ANIMALS

Human trade brought the Silk Road into being, but animals kept it running. Without the camels, horses, donkeys and oxen that carried the merchandise, and the livestock that helped to feed and clothe those who lived along the trade routes and kept them open, the Silk Road would not have thrived as it did. It was the desire for the legendary 'blood-sweating' horses of the Ferghana Valley that drove the first deals along the true Silk Road, and the exchange of Chinese silk for Central Asian horses underpinned much of the Silk Road economy.

Despite the obvious importance of trade – particularly in sustaining the oasis outposts in the arid regions of Central Asia – nomadic pastoralism represented the predominant form of economic activity across the region. The economic and social life of the nomads revolved around their livestock, which provided food in the form of meat and dairy products, and a wide range of other basics such as wool and leather from which they made clothes and household items including quilts, pillows and mattresses.

Nomadic and settled lifestyles were largely interdependent. The nomads relied on settled people for goods that they didn't produce themselves, including grain, tea and manufactured items such as garments, porcelain, weapons and riding tack. These they acquired through a mixture of trade, tribute exchanges and raids on oasis settlements and trade caravans. Oasis communities practised limited stockbreeding, so they relied on the nomads for animals and animal products – horses, meat, milk, leather and untanned animal skins, and wool – which they often obtained in organized oasis bazaars. Nomads also traded livestock – mostly cattle and horses – at special trade fairs set up at border outposts by the Chinese.

The Silk Road, both overland and maritime, and its predecessors were the conduits for the dissemination of many domestic animals from their points of origin. The Maritime Silk Roads in particular

Two Turkmen nomads converse beside a grazing horse in this 15th-century picture. The horses of Central Asia were much larger than those found in China, and the exchange of silk for horses was the foundation for wider Eurasian trade.

were a key mechanism in the spread of a number of domestic and pest animals around the Indian Ocean, bringing Zebu cattle, chickens, rats and mice to Africa, for example.

HORSES

Together with the camel, the horse was a key ingredient in the development and ongoing success of the Silk Road. Horses played a vital role in transportation, communication, trade and warfare, and constituted a precious export commodity. Indeed, the exchange of steppe horses for Chinese silk formed a significant proportion of trade along the Silk Road, continuing until the mid-19th century.

It's unclear when horses were domesticated, but it's believed that the process began in around 3500BCE on the Eurasian steppe. By the end of the third millennium BCE, domestic horses had spread west to lowland Mesopotamia and east to China.

Detail from an 18th-century painted silk scroll depicting Qing-dynasty horses being caught in preparation for a journey with the Qianlong Emperor.

Horseback riding, which dates back to around the ninth century BCE, provided the impetus for the switch from settled agriculture to nomadic pastoralism on the steppe. The development of equestrian skills, in particular mounted archery, eventually gave the steppe peoples a decisive edge in warfare. Indeed, the transition to horse-based warfare was an important turning point in the history of Central Asia.

Up until around 300BCE, the Chinese had paid little attention to their horses, using them mainly for basic transport and farming. However, as China's nomadic neighbours began to build cavalry-based armies, it was forced to learn the ways of mounted warfare. Although it met with some early military success, it quickly became clear that to be truly effective, it would need larger horses.

Hearing from the Western Regions of the Ferghana Valley's 'heavenly horses', the Han Emperor resolved to bolster his armies with these superior beasts, achieving his goal in 102BCE when General Li Guangli returned with 1,000 horses after defeating the rulers of Dayuan. With his newly-strengthened armies, Emperor Wudi was able to wrest control of the Western Regions from the nomadic Xiongnu and make the region's kingdoms his vassals. They were forced to pay heavy tribute in the form of thousands of horses and to deliver further mounts on an annual basis. China's expansion into the steppe also provided access to better pastureland, as did the widespread planting of the newly acquired alfalfa, allowing it to further bolster its herds.

The Horses that Sweat Blood

Stories of 'blood-sweating' horses may sound fanciful, but there is apparently truth in the tales. Central Asian horses are often infested by a parasite that burrows under the skin around their shoulders, producing small nodules. When the horses sustain a long, hard gallop, the nodules burst and bleed, giving the illusion that they are sweating blood.

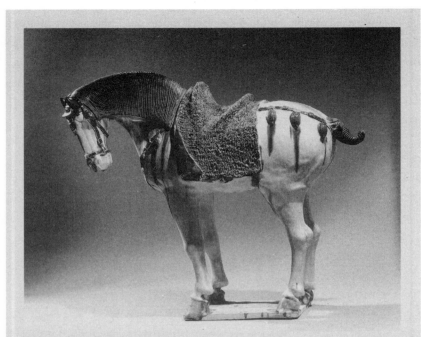

The famed heavenly horses that 'sweated blood' were immortalized in Chinese literature, paintings, and pottery. Statuettes of these horses, such as this one from the Tang dynasty, were sometimes buried with their owners.

However, China was unable to become self-sufficient in horses and was always reliant on the nomadic steppe peoples to keep its armies supplied with mounts. For warfare, communications and transport, the country needed several hundred thousand horses, which meant tens of thousands of new mounts each year to maintain its herds. This put the Chinese at a disadvantage, and the various Central Asian powers from which it sourced its horses often took advantage of the situation, effectively extorting large quantities of silk in exchange for horses. Such was the demand for high-quality mounts that horse breeding became an important economic activity in many regions along the Silk Road.

Like the Chinese, the Mughal Empire on the Indian subcontinent needed foreign horses to uphold its rule because its land was unsuited to raising high-quality steeds. During the late 17th century, about 25,000 Central Asian horses were delivered to India each year; by the 18th century, that figure had risen to as many as 100,000. From the 15th to the 17th centuries, Russia, too, relied on shipments of tens of thousands of Central Asian horses to keep its armies supplied with mounts.

The Mongols' Equine Empire

Horses made possible the inception of nomadic empires, the greatest of which was the Mongol Empire. The Mongols controlled some of the best pasturelands of the north, on which they grazed large numbers of high-quality horses, and more importantly, they knew how to use those horses to support their own society and for warfare.

The close connection between nomads and their mounts was a key factor in their mastery of cavalry warfare. Children learned to ride and use a bow from a very young age. The practice of hunting from horseback led to the development of skills such as the ability to accurately shoot arrows at full gallop. This superior horsemanship meant that the Mongols were extremely mobile, capable of mounting bewildering flank attacks and encirclements. Their composite bows had a range of about 75 m (245 ft), which gave them a significant advantage over their rivals, whose bows' range was closer to 50 m (165 ft).

Although the Mongols' horses weren't particularly large, they were hardy, could travel long distances without tiring and with little food and water, and, crucially, they could survive the harsh winters thanks to their ability to find food under the ice and snow that often blanketed the steppe. While on a military campaign, a Mongol typically took not just a primary warhorse, but also several reserve horses that were used to give the main mount a break after hard use. This allowed troops to move more quickly and helped to keep their mounts fresh. The spare mounts could even be used as food if required. However, the nomads' reliance on horses was one factor that limited the effectiveness of their armies, with the availability of pasturage constraining their size and the amount of time they could spend in a given region.

A Mongol horse archer with a composite bow from the 13th century. Mounted archery provided a great advantage to the steppe peoples, who used their mobility and superior horsemanship to overwhelm their opponents.

CAMELS

With a range of adaptations that suited them to desert life, camels were indispensable for traders wishing to cross the arid regions at the eastern end of the Silk Road as it passed through the Taklamakan Desert and into China, not to mention the waterless expanses of the Arabian Peninsula and Mongolia's Gobi Desert. In the southwest of

Central Asia, the one-humped camel (dromedary) was predominant, whereas in the more northerly or mountainous regions, and along the eastern trade routes, the two-humped (Bactrian) camel was more common.

Camels can survive on extremely meagre food rations, subsisting on scrub and thorn bushes – or even on no food at all by drawing energy from their humps. They are also renowned for their ability to survive on tiny amounts of water; a fully-laden camel can travel for a week or more without drinking. Their broad, padded feet help them to keep their balance on rocky paths and walk across sand without sinking. Long, heavy eyelashes, bushy eyebrows, small, fur-lined ears and nostrils that can shrink to a narrow slit help to keep dust and sand at bay. Camels can also endure the extremes of temperature characteristic of desert environments. In this regard, the Bactrian had an advantage over the dromedary as a Silk Road beast of burden, since its shaggy winter coat enabled it to cross high mountain passes that would have defeated the dromedary.

Bactrian camels were adaptable for use on the Silk Road as pack animals in both desert areas and high mountains. They also provided milk, meat and wool.

When it came to Silk Road trade, camels were very cost-efficient compared to carts, which require good-quality roads and a support network for the animals used to pull them, including more regular watering points and access to fodder. Camels could also carry substantial loads – in the region of 200–250 kg (440–550 lb), much more than a horse or donkey – and travel 40 km (25 miles) in a day.

GOATS

Goats are the most adaptable and geographically widespread of all the livestock species. From the very beginning, when nomadic herders were first moving into Central Asia, goats would have been in the herds they travelled with, and they remained popular among livestock herders along the Silk Road. Hardy and willing to eat just about anything, goats are multi-purpose animals that supply fibre from hair and sinews, milk, meat and hides, as well as dung for fuel.

Although goat wool was used to produce textiles for thousands of years, it wasn't until the 14th or 15th century that an industry was created to exploit the longer, smoother and straighter wool of the cashmere goat. Cashmere wool eventually became an important trade commodity, particularly after it was discovered by Europeans at the end of the 18th century and became popular with the upper classes.

YAKS

When traders needed to cross the highest passes in the Pamirs and the Hindu Kush, they were often forced to hire yaks. Known as 'ships of the Tibetan plateau', yaks are valued for their sure-footed capabilities in carrying large loads over long distances. Although large and bulky, they are safer than horses for riding on steep, rocky slopes and, being adapted to high altitudes, they can cope better when the air gets thin or the weather closes in.

Dried yak dung is the only available fuel on the treeless Tibetan plateau, and its availability has even been suggested as a potentially critical factor for colonization of the high plateau. Yaks also provide sustenance in the form of their high-fat milk – which is turned into butter and cheese, yoghurt and whey – and occasionally meat, blood and fat. The butter was burned in lamps. Their coats have long, strong outer hairs, which were used to make ropes, tent cloth, pack bags and ornamentation in the form of hair extensions. The fine, woolly underhair was turned into yarn, felt, clothing and blankets.

SHEEP

Sheep breeding was the primary economic activity of many nomads living along the Silk Road. Although they usually had mixed livestock of sheep, goats, cattle and horses, sheep typically made up the majority of the herds, which could number in the tens of thousands. As well as being kept for meat and milk, sheep provided

The heavy build and long hair of Tibetan yaks, which have adapted to thrive in the thinner air at high altitudes, made them ideal for carrying large loads across rocky mountain passes.

wool, which was an important Silk Road trade commodity, as were woollen textiles and sheepskins. The wool was also turned into felt, which lined the nomads' tents to provide insulation and was used for clothing (including boot linings), saddle pads and furnishings.

The most popular breed along the Silk Road was the Karakul sheep, named for a city in what is now Uzbekistan. Developed in the desert regions of Central Asia in around 140BCE, Karakul sheep are renowned for their ability to survive extremely harsh living conditions. They are excellent foragers, able to graze marginal land in which ordinary sheep wouldn't survive, can subsist on scant food thanks to their ability to store fat in their tails, and can withstand extremes of both hot and cold.

CROPS

When nomadic shepherds opened some of the first links between eastern and western Asia nearly 5,000 years ago, they began sharing domesticated crops from opposite sides of the continent. Wheat and barley from the Fertile Crescent (in the Middle East) and broomcorn millet from China have been recovered from ancient nomadic campsites in what is now Kazakhstan. These exchanges represent the very beginnings of the Silk Road.

Movement of plants along the Silk Road took many forms. At first, it was mostly swapping among agro-pastoralists. Pastoral nomads would also have been transporting foods and agricultural species. Then came trade, some of which was about fulfilling needs, but some was about luxuries and exotic goods craved by elites. And then there were diplomatic visits, when exotic plants and animals were given as gifts and tributes.

Initial opening up of the 'true' Silk Road during the Han dynasty led to a flood of new crops arriving in China, including apples, pears, cherries, plums, peaches, cucumbers, walnuts, sesame, pomegranates, onions, garlic and grapes. The next major flowering of trade, during the Tang dynasty, saw the introduction to China of spinach, black pepper, dates, lettuce, luffa, watermelons and pistachios. Bananas and mangoes arrived from South and Southeast Asia.

The Silk Road was also a conduit for the transmission of farming technology – in the form of tools such as the plough, scythe, sickle and millstone; in the form of knowledge of how to cultivate the new crops, such as grafting, which was probably developed in China or Central Asia; and in the form of the irrigation technology required for farming in the arid regions through which the Silk Road passed. The *karez* underground irrigation system used around Turfan in the north of the Tarim Basin was probably a local version of *qanat*, acquired via the Silk Road from ancient Persia (where it was developed in the first millennium BCE) – both techniques are still in use today. During the Han dynasty, the *tuntian* system, whereby Chinese Silk Road garrisons doubled as agricultural communities, also brought irrigation to the Tarim, along with crops such as grains, mulberries, hemp and grapes.

In general, traditional oasis farmers cultivated a mixture of wheat, barley, millet, cotton and rice. They also bred silkworms, grew a variety of vegetables and fruit, and grew grapes for wine. The grains were not just food or trade commodities: in many parts of the Silk Road they also became a form of currency. Grain – particularly millet, but also wheat – was used to pay taxes; monasteries accepted it as tribute or as payment for activities such as printing images of Buddha, and they often 'loaned' some of their surplus to farmers, who used it as seed for the next season's crop.

Not all movement of plants along the Silk Roads was conscious. There is evidence that weeds also spread along the different trade routes. For example, horse purslanes and buttonweeds probably moved from South Asia to Southeast Asia and East Africa via Indian Ocean trade.

Maritime trade had significant long-term impacts on some regions. Grains such as sorghum and pearl and finger millet, along with pulses including cowpea and hyacinth bean, were transported from Africa to India, where they became some of the country's staple crops. Trade along the Maritime Silk Road also brought rice, mung beans, sesame, citrus and Asian millet varieties to East Africa, while during the medieval period a range of new crops came to Egypt from South and Southeast Asia, including rice, aubergines, citrus, taro, bananas and sugarcane. At the same time, Arab traders introduced to Europe a wide range of exotic spices, as well as sorghum, buckwheat, aubergine, citrus, sugarcane and mango.

WHEAT

It's thought that cultivated common wheat originated in the Middle East and was carried along what would become the Silk Road into China, where it became the dominant crop in the dry-land agriculture of northern China. As it made the long journey from its point of origin, wheat adapted to a diversity of local environments, with the help of farmers using selective breeding. Moving east, farmers selected strains that produced smaller grains, which were more suited to a Chinese cuisine that prepared them by boiling or steaming the whole grains. On its westward journey, the grains grew larger, because Europeans traditionally ground wheat for flour. In China wheat was initially a delicacy reserved for the aristocracy, but during the Han dynasty the development of water- and animal-powered mills saw an increase in the production of flour, which was used to make what are now typical northern Chinese dishes such as noodles and dumplings.

MILLET

Along with rice, foxtail and broomcorn millet appear to be the oldest cereals cultivated in China. Both were domesticated there, broomcorn millet in about 8000BCE and foxtail millet around 6500BCE. Millets thrive in hot, arid climates; they are fast-growing and drought-tolerant, which meant that they were well-adapted for growing in Central Asia, by both settled and nomadic farmers, providing a low-risk, low-investment crop for marginal agricultural areas. They were also used to brew alcohol.

HEMP

Hemp was one of the earliest crops grown in China, domesticated about 5,000 years ago. It was commonly grown as a seed crop and was a staple of the Chinese diet until the tenth century. The plant was also used in traditional medicines, and its fibres were used to make paper and to spin yarn and weave cloth; in early Chinese society, hemp textile was the main cloth worn. By the Tang dynasty, hemp was widely traded along the Silk Road.

COTTON

While there's an obvious emphasis on westward trade along the Silk Road in Chinese silk, eastward trade in Indian cotton textiles was also significant. Indian cotton goods reached China's Western Regions not long after the start of the first century CE, and by the fourth and fifth centuries, cotton was being produced there. China itself didn't cultivate cotton or produce cotton cloth in significant quantities until the late 13th and early 14th centuries, and even then it continued to import Indian cotton, partly because the variety of cotton grown in China was of inferior quality to the Indian varieties.

For centuries, Indian cotton dominated Indian Ocean trade along the Maritime Silk Roads. The cloth was very popular in ancient Rome – valued almost as highly as Chinese silk – and Roman traders bought it in huge quantities from ports on the Red Sea.

ALFALFA

Alfalfa or lucerne, a member of the pea family, is the oldest crop grown solely for feeding animals. It was originally found in mountainous regions of southwestern Asia and was probably domesticated around 9,000 years ago in what is now Iran. Alfalfa's popularity as an animal feed stems from its high yield and high nutritional value – it's both high in protein and highly digestible. When the Chinese envoy Zhang Qian travelled through the Ferghana Valley in around 130BCE, he took note not only of the powerful horses there but also of their high-quality fodder: alfalfa. Many accounts

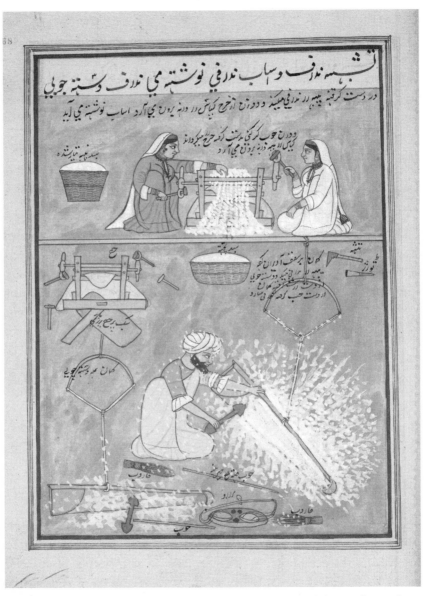

The invention of mechanical devices such as the cotton gin led to widespread use of cotton, as fibres could be more easily separated, disentangled and cleaned. This 19th-century watercolour depicts Indian workers ginning (top) and carding (bottom).

suggest that it was Zhang who brought alfalfa seeds back to the Han court following his long journey into the Western Regions (along with grapes, pomegranates, walnuts, coriander and flax seeds), but it appears more likely that while Zhang brought back first-hand accounts of these crops, it fell to other envoys to actually procure them for the Han court. Regardless of how it reached China, alfalfa was soon under cultivation, first in palace gardens and then more widely for food for the herds of heavenly horses.

TEA

It's thought that tea was first domesticated in southwest China's Yunnan province during the Shang dynasty, when it was brewed as a medicinal drink. Although there's evidence that tea was being carried along the Silk Road at least as far as Tibet by around 200CE, significant trade isn't thought to have taken place until the Tang dynasty.

Prior to the 19th century, tea was usually sold and traded in brick form. Dried and ground tea-leaves were compressed to form bricks that were then left to cure, dry and age. More compact than loose-leaf tea and less susceptible to damage, the bricks were sometimes sewn into yak skins in order to withstand battering and bad weather. The bricks were sometimes used as a form of currency for bartering. Their durability is evidenced by the fact that during the early 20th century ancient bricks were regularly uncovered from the sands of the Taklamakan Desert and sold in local markets.

GRAPES

Wild grapevines are found in many different regions, but the main species used for table grapes and for making wine originated in the Near East and was domesticated in the Mediterranean. Viniculture in Central Asia developed under Hellenistic influence: northern India and Central Asia were introduced to wine culture by Alexander the Great's armies. Grapes were well adapted to the oasis environments and were widely grown in the Tarim Basin by the late Bronze Age.

Grapevines were introduced to China from Central Asia during the second century BCE, after Zhang Qian noted people making and drinking wine during his travels through the Western Regions. At first the Chinese only used the grapes for eating – sometimes drying them to make raisins and sultanas. It wasn't until the Tang dynasty, when China conquered areas of the Western Regions where wine was made, that Chinese viniculture began to develop, although alcohol made from grains such as rice, sorghum and millet was still preferred.

MULBERRIES

The mulberry tree is uniquely entwined with the Silk Road. Silkworms feed only on the leaves of one species of mulberry – the white mulberry; it takes 200 kg (440 lb) of leaves to produce 1 kg (2.2 lb) of silk thread. As silk became a valuable trade commodity and diplomatic tool – and indeed, a *de facto* currency – its production took on a central importance to successive Chinese dynasties, so mulberry trees came to be planted extensively across China and beyond, including in many of the oasis settlements along the Silk Road.

APPLES

All of the world's apple varieties share a common ancestor – a wild apple native to what is now Kazakhstan. As this medium-sized, mushy, rather tasteless fruit spread east and west along the Silk Road, trees grew from dropped seeds and hybridized with other wild apple varieties. On the journey east, the crosses yielded the ancestors of the soft dessert apples cultivated in China today; on the westward journey, they bred with crab apples, eventually becoming the crisp, sweet apple that we in the West know and love today.

RHUBARB

There are several different species of rhubarb, all of which are native to a broad area of eastern Asia. One species, found in mountainous areas of western China, was being cultivated by the Chinese for medicinal purposes as early as 2700BCE. The plant's roots were valued for their purgative properties, but were also prescribed for an extremely wide variety of ailments. Indeed, ground-up rhubarb root was considered to be one of the most powerful and useful drugs of its time and was one of the first Chinese medicines to be imported by the West.

During the first five centuries CE, the Sassanian Empire controlled the trade in rhubarb along the Silk Road; however, it didn't become properly established until the 13th and 14th centuries. By the 15th century, the Timurids in Samarkand were the main supplier of rhubarb to the Islamic world, North Africa and Europe, with about 500 tonnes of Chinese rhubarb imported into the great trading city each year. During the 17th and 18th centuries, Chinese rhubarb was one of the most prominent medicinal plants in the world; the drug was so highly sought after that it was three times as expensive as opium.

DISEASE

Where people go, disease follows. One of the unpleasant side-effects of long-distance trade is the spread of disease. As traders made their way back and forth along the Silk Road, they acted as vectors for a number of infectious diseases, including the Black Death, measles, smallpox, diphtheria, leprosy and possibly even anthrax.

Several factors combined to promote the transmission of disease along the Silk Road. The growth of agriculture brought people into closer contact with animals – be it livestock in the fields or rodents in the grain stores – increasing the likelihood that diseases would jump across the species barrier; the rudimentary nature of hygiene and medical treatment did little to stop diseases from spreading; many of the diseases were novel to people living along the Silk Road, so there was little natural immunity; people regularly gathered in large groups – at markets and in caravanserais – increasing the opportunities to transfer disease; and, of course, traders were travelling long distances, hastening the spread of disease and potentially bringing pathogens to what would otherwise be isolated communities.

It was not just human diseases. Animals in trade caravans and nomads' herds would have acted as carriers for livestock diseases that could be potentially devastating for small farming communities. It appears likely that anthrax was spread in this way. Crop diseases, too, piggybacked on Silk Road trade. Barley stripe mosaic virus, for example, originated in the Middle East or North Africa, and spread to East Asia along historical trade routes during the late medieval period. Similarly, apple scab disease first emerged in Central Asia before being introduced to Europe along the Silk Road.

Nor was it just the overland Silk Road. The maritime routes were also implicated in the spread of disease. For example, it's

Smallpox was one of many serious diseases carried along the Silk Road. This 17th-century Turkish miniature shows medicines being prepared for a patient suffering from smallpox.

thought that leprosy entered China via both the overland routes from Central Asia and the maritime routes through the ports of Guangzhou and Ningbo. Smallpox, too, is thought to have spread across Eurasia via both maritime and overland Silk Roads. Interestingly, a method of combating the disease, known as variolation – a precursor to modern vaccination, whereby ground-up scabs from smallpox sufferers were blown up the nostrils of healthy people in order to confer immunity to the disease – was also spread along Silk Road. First developed in China during the 15th century, the technique eventually reached Turkey, where it was observed by the wife of the British Ambassador to the Ottoman Empire, Lady Mary Wortley Montagu, who subsequently introduced it to England.

In some cases, diseases carried along the Silk Road turned into epidemics that had a significant, often devastating, impact on societies and empires. For instance, the Antonine Plague of 165–180CE, which killed about 10 per cent of the population of the Roman Empire, severely affected Indo-Roman trade relations in the Indian Ocean and may well have hastened the empire's demise. The cause of the plague is unknown; measles and smallpox have both been blamed, with the latter the more likely culprit.

Between 249 and 262, the Roman Empire was again visited by a pandemic. The cause of the so-called Plague of Cyprian is also unknown, with smallpox, influenza and a viral haemorrhagic fever similar to the Ebola virus all being blamed. At the height of the outbreak, 5,000 people a day were said to be dying in Rome.

And during the sixth to eighth centuries, the Byzantine Empire was laid low by the Justinian Plague – the first recorded incidence of bubonic plague – which caused the deaths of an estimated 25–50 million people over two centuries of recurrence. It's thought that the disease may have originated in either India or China and was carried along the Maritime Silk Road to Constantinople via Ethiopia in fleas living on black rats that stowed aboard merchant ships.

However, the most devastating of the pandemics to have affected the Silk Road – and to have used it as a transmission route – was the Black Death. This was caused by the bubonic plague, a bacterial disease that is spread mainly by infected fleas. It's thought to have originated in the Central Asian steppe, before being carried along the Silk Road to an Italian trading station in Crimea called Kaffa (now known as Feodosiya), which was under siege by the Mongols. In autumn 1346, plague broke out among the Mongols and then made its way into the town (the Mongol army actually catapulted infected corpses over the city walls in order to infect the inhabitants). The following spring, the Italian merchants fled the city aboard their ships – ships that were carrying black rats that were carrying fleas infected with the plague. These vessels called in at several ports before returning to their hometowns of Genoa and Venice. From each of those trading hubs, the disease spread further – into North Africa and the Middle East, and across Europe.

The original outbreak petered out during the 1350s, but the plague continued to reappear every few generations for several centuries. Estimates of the total death toll vary, but as much as 60 per cent of Europe's population may have died – in the region of 50 million people. Across Eurasia as a whole, casualties are thought to have numbered between 75 and 200 million people. As with previous pandemics, the Black Death had a devastating impact on the societies affected, leading to a series of religious, social and economic upheavals with profound effects on the course of Eurasian history.

In modern times, the ancient Silk Road has once again become a route for disease transmission. Overland drug-trafficking routes that overlap the Silk Road now connect Afghanistan and Central Asia's former Soviet republics with China, Russia and Western Europe. Research has shown that HIV and hepatitis C are being disseminated along these routes.

Silk Road Disease

A multi-system auto-immune disorder that manifests as a triad of symptoms consisting of recurrent eye inflammation and oral and genital ulcers, Behçet's disease was first described by Hippocrates 2,500 years ago. However, it wasn't properly 'discovered' until the 20th century, when a Turkish dermatologist, Hulusi Behçet, recognized and reported it in 1937. The disease has a worldwide distribution, but is most commonly seen among populations living along the historic Silk Road – hence it's also known as Silk Road Disease. Its prevalence is far higher in Turkey than in any other nation: about one in 250 people in Turkey have Behçet's disease.

Susceptibility to the disease appears to have a genetic component, which probably spread along the Silk Road, although the origin of the illness and the direction of travel are still unknown. This case is interesting because it's not the disease itself that has spread but the increased susceptibility – that is, it's a case of genetic change rather than pathogenic transmission.

— 10 —
ART ALONG
THE SILK ROAD

The transmission of ideas along the Silk Road is perhaps best represented by the regular sharing of artistic styles and motifs that took place over the centuries. Interactions between Hellenistic, Iranian, Indian and Chinese artistic styles are evident in everything from paintings and murals, statuary, porcelain and glass to textiles (in the form of motifs on silks and in carpets and rugs), jade carvings and metalwork. Each time an artistic tradition spread out across Eurasia it took on local and regional characteristics, leading to a complex melange of styles.

Movement of artistic forms and techniques along the traditional trade routes was intimately connected to the exchange of ideas, technology and, perhaps most importantly, religious beliefs. A significant proportion of the art of the Silk Road was religious in origin, with an emphasis on the devotional art of Buddhism and Islam, the two most widely practised religions in the territories through which its various branches passed.

Graeco-Buddhist art is probably one of the most vivid examples of these artistic interactions. Buddhist sculptures can be found scattered along the Silk Road from Iran to China and on to Korea and Japan. Towards the end of the first millennium BCE, as Buddhism spread from India into Afghanistan, it was introduced to the remains of Alexander the Great's armies, particularly in the region of Gandhara (in modern-day northern Pakistan). The local Buddhist art soon began to take on traditional Greek sculptural elements, such as highly realistic portraiture, a penchant for faces with a subtle smile and a particular standing posture with the hips thrust forward. Known as Gandharan art, this Graeco-Buddhist style had a widespread influence on art across Central Asia. A classic example is the giant standing Buddhas of the Bamiyan Valley in Afghanistan, which were destroyed by the Taliban Islamic fundamentalists in 2001. The Gandharan style reached China during the Tang dynasty, transforming sculpture there, both Buddhist and secular, bringing a notable increase in realism.

Buddhist art also influenced Chinese landscape painting and the miniaturist art of Persia. Artists creating the large murals depicting scenes from Buddha's life developed conventions for the background landscapes that were later absorbed by secular painters in China. These same conventions – notably the silhouettes of trees on mountain ridges, the layered-plane treatment of mountains and the way in which clouds and fire were depicted – also made their way west, where they can be seen in the miniatures used to illuminate books in Persia during the 14th to 16th centuries. And the halo, a symbol indelibly linked with Christian art, was introduced to the

The giant Buddhas of the Bamiyan Valley in Afghanistan were classic examples of Gandharan art, but they were destroyed by Islamic fundamentalists in 2001.

Byzantine world during the fifth century via Buddhist and Persian pictorial art. Halos can be seen in murals in the Mogao Caves, in Persian representations of kings and gods, in Mughal book illuminations and on Kushan coins.

Other aspects of Greek art also travelled widely. During the second century CE, the floral scroll, a Greek artistic motif, made its way from the Hellenistic regions to the Tarim Basin; between the fourth and sixth centuries it was adopted by Chinese ceramic artists. And Greek gods such as Herakles and Boreas were often used as the basis for the depiction of Buddhist deities.

The Islamization of the Silk Road, which began at the start of the eighth century, brought another wave of artistic influence. Islam's prohibition on representations of people and animals meant that Islamic art tended to focus more on calligraphic, geometric and

A golden Sogdian silk, probably from Bukhara (in modern Uzbekistan), shows the distinctive Persian feature of two animals – in this case, lions – facing each other within a circle of dots.

other non-representational artistic motifs, such as intertwining tendrils known as arabesques. All of these turned up on carpets and on the glazed tilework of mosques. When the Islamic Abbasid Empire began to break up into smaller states towards the end of the first millennium, each of the new states developed its own artistic styles.

Textiles are another art form that saw styles, motifs and techniques travel in both directions along the Silk Road. During the Tang dynasty, Chinese weavers began to incorporate the typical Persian roundel figure, which often featured two animals facing each other within a circle of dots, into their designs, partly to cater to the export market and partly because the style had become popular in China. Ikat, a cloth that is patterned by weaving previously tie-dyed threads, originated in Indonesia and India, and spread to Persia, Central Asia, western China and Japan.

Some of the artistic exchanges that took place had a mercantile angle to them. Local artists were often influenced by foreign designs brought in by traders, leading to a blending of styles. Imported motifs might be incorporated into products destined for export – an attempt to appeal to the predilections of the goods' recipients. For example, Chinese potters often used motifs that were popular in the Middle East, such as tulips, pomegranates and Arabic calligraphy, on porcelain for export. The motifs would then begin to appear in products for local sale.

The Mystery of the Three Hares

One of the more puzzling of the motifs to have spread out along the Silk Road is the symbol of the three (or sometimes four) hares, which features three hares or rabbits chasing each other in a circle, usually in a clockwise direction. The symbol has a threefold rotational symmetry, with each of the ears shared by two hares, so only three ears are shown.

Its first known use was in the Mogao Caves near Dunhuang. During the Sui and Tang dynasties, the symbol was painted in the centre of the ceilings of at least 17 caves, typically surrounded by large lotus petals. In each case, it forms the focal point of a painted canopy that covers the entire ceiling. However, it's thought to be unlikely that the motif originated in Dunhuang – it's more likely to have come from Mesopotamia, or perhaps the Hellenistic world, and spread via Sogdian or Sassanian travellers.

During the Mongol era, the image spread more widely. Examples of objects bearing the symbol include a 13th- or early-14th-century Iranian box; an ancient Islamic-made reliquary from southern Russia; 13th-century Mongol metalwork; a copper coin found in Iran, dating from 1281; 13th-century Middle Eastern and Central Asian ceramics; and a 12th-century Islamic glass medallion. Then, during the late medieval period, it turns up in Europe, appearing in Christian churches, particularly in France and Germany but most commonly in Devon, England; on Jewish headstones in Ukraine; and in 17th- and 18th-century German synagogues. It's unknown what the motif represents or how it made its way from Central Asia to medieval Britain, but it's thought to have spread out of Asia as a design incorporated into expensive Oriental ceramics, silk cloth and metalwork.

Much of the trade along the Silk Road took the form of luxury objects coveted by wealthy elites, and foreign works of art were among the more popular of these. Such pieces would frequently be copied by local artisans, potentially inspiring new artistic modes. While this trade was one of the major modes of transmission of artworks and artistic ideas, the movement of artists themselves was clearly also important. Professional artists were often commissioned

An illustration from Zafarnama *or the Book of Victory (1467) depicts Timur at the time of his accession. When he made Samarkand his capital, he brought artists from across Asia to make it the most beautiful city in the world.*

to work in foreign countries by local rulers, religious institutions and other wealthy patrons. In some cases, however, this movement wasn't of the artists' volition. When Timur rose to power and made Samarkand his capital, he set about turning the city into the most beautiful in the world. In order to achieve this goal, he brought artists and craftspeople to Samarkand in their thousands, having captured them during his rampages across Asia. The Mongols, too, had a habit of shifting artists and artworks between China and the Middle East.

Blue-and-white Porcelain

The history of blue-and-white porcelain is a textbook example of the back-and-forth cross-cultural exchanges that took place along the Silk Roads. From about the ninth century, Chinese porcelain started to make its way to the Islamic world, mostly via the Maritime Silk Road. Not long afterwards, Islamic potters began decorating tin-glazed vessels with cobalt. These items, as well as the cobalt itself, were brought to coastal cities in China by Muslim merchants, again mostly via the Maritime Silk Road. Towards the end of 13th century, potters in southern China started to use cobalt blue to decorate white porcelain items, which soon

This blue-and-white porcelain vase, dating from the Ming dynasty, was modelled on the shape of a bronze altar vessel. Cobalt was imported from the Middle East to make the distinctive blue colour.

became extremely popular in the Middle East. Then, towards the end of the 15th century, potters in the Turkish town of Iznik began to produce blue-and-white ceramics bearing designs influenced by the Ottoman court in Istanbul.

The Mogao Caves

Dug into the east-facing cliffs above the Dachuan River, about 25 km (16 miles) southeast of the oasis town of Dunhuang, in what is now Gansu province, China, the Mogao Caves comprise the world's largest and most richly endowed collection of Buddhist art. Also known as the Caves of the Thousand Buddhas, the 492 grottoes house about 45,000 sq m (484,000 sq ft) of murals and more than 2,000 painted sculptures.

Construction of the caves is thought to have begun in 366 and ceased during the 14th century. At first, they were dug out for Buddhist hermits to use for meditation and worship. However, as monasteries were established nearby, the caves became a popular site of pilgrimage and worship by Buddhists of all types. Patrons such as clergy, local rulers, foreign dignitaries, Chinese emperors, merchants, military officers and even local community groups paid to have caves dug out and murals painted inside (with the art sometimes incorporating a small image of the patrons themselves). Before painting, the rough walls were prepared with a mixture of mud, straw and reeds, and then covered with a lime paste. The murals were painted with mineral pigments and gold and silver leaf.

This painting from Dunhuang c.875 depicts a bodhisattva leading a woman to the Pure Land, indicating a change from earlier depictions of Jakata tales.

These caves contain an unmatched record of the evolution of Buddhist art in northwestern China. The murals' artistic style is a melding of Chinese, Indian, Gandharan, Turkish and Tibetan influences, with the styles of different regions having more or less impact over time. Older paintings have elements that reflect Indian and Western influences, while those painted during the Tang dynasty were more influenced by the styles of the Chinese imperial court. The subsequent loss of Chinese control of the Western Regions saw Dunhuang become more isolated, and the paintings took on a unique local style.

Dunhuang's murals also reflect the way in which Buddhist beliefs in the region changed with the centuries. Early caves mostly contain depictions of Jataka tales (stories about the many incarnations of the Buddha) but from the Tang dynasty onwards the paintings begin to show scenes of Paradise, reflecting a switch to so-called Pure Land Buddhism, which is built around a striving to be reborn on another plane – the 'Pure Land'.

As trade along the Silk Road dwindled during the Ming dynasty, Dunhuang slowly became depopulated, but the caves were still visited by pilgrims and local worshippers, before the arrival of Western explorers at the end of the 19th century brought renewed attention to the site. In 1987, the caves were inscribed on the World Heritage list and they are now a popular tourist destination. Much of the art has been digitally recorded, and is thus viewable worldwide, with a measure of protection against future physical decay.

— II —
THE REBIRTH
OF THE SILK ROADS

In November 2013, Chinese president Xi Jinping announced a proposal to, in effect, reopen the ancient Silk Roads. China hopes that its Belt and Road Initiative (BRI) will kickstart a new era of globalization by creating free-trade corridors that link China to the rest of Asia and Europe, Africa and Latin America. Encompassing both land (the 'belt', as in the Silk Road Economic Belt) and maritime routes (the 'road', as in the Maritime Silk Road), the plan is ostensibly to improve global trade relationships, primarily through investment in energy and transport infrastructure.

Taken together, the BRI's many constituent parts represent one of the largest infrastructure projects in human history. Among the developments already under way are railways in Indonesia, Iran, Turkey, Nigeria and Serbia, ports in Pakistan, Sri Lanka and Myanmar, roads in Albania, Kyrgyzstan and Cambodia, a bridge in Russia, dams in Cambodia and Pakistan, a pipeline in Azerbaijan and an industrial park in Belarus. There are also hydropower plants in Uganda, Georgia and Indonesia, wind farms in Pakistan and a solar power plant in Kazakhstan. To take just one example, the 414-kilometre (257-mile) China–Laos rail link is set to be the longest railway in Asia outside China, with 72 tunnels with a total length of 198 km (123 miles) and 167 bridges with a total length of 62 km (39 miles). The project has the potential to turn landlocked Laos into a land-linked hub.

The benefits for China and its trading partners could be enormous. The area covered by the initiative is home to more than two thirds of the world's population, produces just over a third of global GDP and

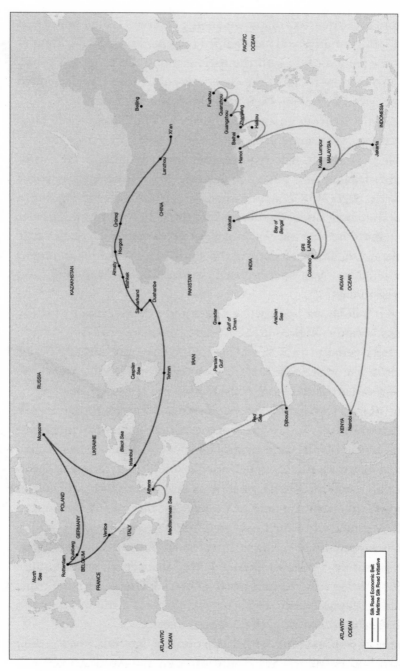

Designed to enhance connectivity among countries across Eurasia and beyond, China's Belt and Road Initiative is the largest global infrastructure project of modern times.

has about three quarters of known energy reserves. China hopes that by 2025, the initiative will have helped to generate US$2.5 trillion in additional annual trade with the nations along the proposed route, while also helping to boost the economies of China's less-developed border regions by linking them with neighbouring countries.

Success is far from guaranteed, however. The initiative is a huge undertaking, with many projects slated to take place in politically unstable regions. It will require collaboration among numerous countries located alongside the historic Silk Roads and beyond; by March 2020, 138 countries had joined the BRI by signing a memorandum of understanding with China, according to Chinese state media. The physical challenges are also formidable, particularly in Central Asia, home to some of the world's tallest mountain ranges – over which many of the proposed pipelines and road and rail links will need to pass.

And it will be very costly; estimates and announcements for the total cost range as high as US$8 trillion. According to one estimate, 2,951 BRI projects valued at US$3.87 trillion are already under way across the wider Silk Road region, involving 2,630 companies; however, other estimates are considerably more conservative.

One of the most significant beneficiaries is Pakistan, where work is already under way on US$62 billion worth of new roads, pipelines, bridges, power plants, wind farms, factories and other China-backed infrastructure projects grouped together under the China-Pakistan Economic Corridor (CPEC) banner. Designed to link Xinjiang in western China with the port of Gwadar on the Indian Ocean, the CPEC is projected to create up to a million new jobs. At Gwadar, China is reportedly planning to establish an 'international port city' that will feature a purpose-built financial district, an airport and a US$265 million luxury golf resort. There are also reportedly plans to build a 'Chinese-only' township for the half-a-million Chinese nationals who will work in the financial district.

China is also working with Russia on an 'Ice Silk Road', using the so-called Northern Sea Route through the Arctic to connect

China and Europe. Melting of the ice in the Arctic Ocean due to climate change is making this route, which shaves nine to ten days off a journey between China and European markets compared to the traditional routes via the Strait of Malacca and Suez Canal, increasingly viable. China also sees cooperation with Russia as a way of gaining access to Arctic mineral resources, which are also becoming increasingly available due to climate change. The China National Petroleum Corporation (CNPC) and the Silk Road Fund are co-investors with Russia in the Yamal liquid natural gas (LNG) project, which is developing a LNG plant and transport infrastructure, including a seaport and airport in Sabetta on Russia's Yamal Peninsula. In 2018, a Russian tanker loaded with LNG arrived at a Chinese port in Rudong County via the Arctic North-East Passage, the first such shipment to arrive directly from the Russian Arctic by ship.

While the initiative is extremely ambitious, it's also relatively amorphous and opaque; there's no public blueprint for BRI, nor is there a firm timeline or any overarching, centralized day-to-day control. It has even been renamed more than once. And although most of the announced projects have been related to infrastructure development, the BRI is so loosely defined that it has come to include a wide and ever-expanding list of activities that includes fashion shows, concerts, art exhibitions and an alliance of universities. It includes numerous projects that pre-date Xi's 2013 announcement, but omits several similar Chinese-funded projects in non-participant countries. Every Chinese province has its own BRI investment plan, but Chinese cities must apply to be involved.

Similarly, Chinese motivations for the project are manifold. They can, however, be broken down into three main themes. The first is domestic economic development. Over the past few years, China has experienced an overall slowdown in economic growth, which has resulted in a reduction in construction. This has created large overcapacities in labour and the production of commodities such as steel and cement that are required for the construction of hard

Glaciers on the Novaya Zemlya archipelago. China is working with Russia to establish an 'Ice Silk Road' through the Arctic Ocean, made possible due to global warming. If successful, it will offer a much shorter route for trade between the two countries.

infrastructure. By undertaking large infrastructure projects overseas, the Chinese government can effectively export those overcapacities, in the process taking some of the steam out of its economy and heading off potential political problems at home. China also hopes that the BRI will more firmly integrate its western provinces, which have been struggling economically for decades, into the wider Asian economy.

The second element is political. China's investment in other countries can be seen as a way to create political dependencies, a sort of quid pro quo whereby in return for China granting loans for infrastructure projects it in effect buys those countries' loyalty and, crucially, support when it comes to contentious issues such as territorial claims in the South China Sea and human rights.

A perfect example of this can be seen in reactions to China's crackdown on Uighurs and other mostly Muslim ethnic minorities in its vast western border region of Xinjiang. After a series of violent incidents in the region, which Beijing blamed on Uighurs, Chinese officials began to set up internment camps – described as 'vocational education centres' – that estimates suggest now house more than a million Uighurs and other mostly Muslim Turkic-speaking minorities, including ethnic Kazakhs and Kyrgyz.

Although Beijing characterizes the camps as voluntary schools for vocational and anti-extremism training, many observers have linked them to the BRI. Xinjiang is the gateway to Central Asia, where China is involved in numerous large-scale BRI projects, and Pakistan, one of China's key BRI project partners. Three of the six planned BRI economic corridors pass through Xinjiang and a distribution hub is being developed in Khorgos on the Xinjiang–Kazakhstan border. And, obviously, the original ancient Silk Road route to Europe passed through Central Asia, so the region has an important symbolic relevance to the BRI. Hence, it's widely believed that Beijing is going all out to bring the restive region under control, once and for all, in order to reduce the possibility of disruption to its attempts to re-open the ancient trade route.

The crackdown has placed political leaders in the wider region in an awkward position. Although those being caught up in the Chinese dragnet are fellow Muslims, leaders in Central Asia and Pakistan are reluctant to criticize Beijing as they are key recipients of BRI projects and China is an important trade partner. Consequently, they have refrained from publicly criticizing China's behaviour in Xinjiang, despite the growing public discontent within their own countries.

Regional stability is another aspect of this political component. Several volatile regions lie within China's wider neighbourhood and it has been suggested that China views economic development as a way of improving local political stability.

The third element is a re-shaping of China's image, casting it as a good global citizen, contributing to globalization and building capacity in developing nations through infrastructure development.

President Xi has also set his hopes on the BRI helping to restore the dignity of the Chinese nation.

Going beyond these three core motivations, BRI will also potentially offer benefits to China by internationalizing the Chinese currency and improving energy security. About 80 per cent of China's oil imports currently pass through the 2.8-km-wide (1.7 mile) Strait of Malacca, where they are vulnerable to interception by hostile foreign powers. Known as the Malacca Dilemma, this issue is most likely a key motivation for China's push to build pipelines that link it with Central Asia and Pakistan and to establish the Ice Silk Road.

DEBT-TRAP DIPLOMACY

Funding for the BRI mostly takes the form of loans to participating governments – typically on commercial terms. According to RWR Advisory, a Washington-based consultancy, there has been US$461 billion of announced lending by Chinese financial institutions to BRI projects since 2013. Governments are attracted to the loans because of China's promise of non-interference in local politics, its willingness to assume risks that other lenders won't and its less

Cargo ships pass through the Strait of Malacca, one of the world's busiest shipping routes, through which 80 per cent of China's oil imports pass.

stringent requirements for implementing social and environmental safeguards. China is also relatively flexible when it comes to negotiating repayment terms, often signalling a willingness to accept natural resources or equity when loans can't be repaid.

The amount of debt that some countries are taking on has many observers worried, as servicing those debts will potentially leave little for domestic public investment and could push the recipients into default – what's known as debt-trap diplomacy. A policy paper released in 2018 by the US-based Center for Global Development identified eight countries that are at particular risk of debt distress due to lending associated with BRI. These include Laos, where the US$6billion cost of the planned China–Laos railway would represent almost half the country's GDP, and Kyrgyzstan, where public and publicly guaranteed debt amounts to roughly 65 per cent of GDP and 40 per cent of foreign debt is tied up in loans from the state-owned Export-Import Bank of China (China Eximbank). In Macedonia, overall public debt has risen to the point where it almost exceeds national GDP, largely due to Chinese infrastructure financing. If, in the long run, the projects don't make the expected return on investment, many countries will struggle to service their debt. Overall, out of 64 countries that host BRI projects, 20 have already gone into distress and eight are likely to lose their sovereign debt sustainability if they take out further loans.

Should foreign governments default on their loans, there's every chance that China will foreclose on them and seize the properties, as has already begun to happen. Having defaulted on several Chinese loans for infrastructure projects, the Zambian government has had to hand over control of Kenneth Kaunda International Airport in the capital, Lusaka, to Beijing and has reportedly been in talks that could see the total surrender of the state electricity company, ZESCO, and give Chinese companies control of Zambia's copper-mining assets, including the country's third-largest mine, Mopani. Kenya may soon lose control of the Port of Mombasa, the country's largest and most lucrative port, after defaulting on the Chinese loan used to build it. And in Sri Lanka, inability to service the debt on the Magampura Mahinda Rajapaksa Port, which was 85 per cent funded by China Eximbank, forced the government to lease the port to the Chinese state-owned China Merchants Port Holdings Company Limited on a 99-year lease in 2017. And in 2019, Chinese port operators tightened their grip on the Doraleh Container Terminal in Djibouti, where debt to China is equal to nearly 100 per cent of GDP.

In the face of these harsh realities, China is beginning to see significant pushback against many of its BRI projects. In late 2018 and 2019, several BRI partners, including Sri Lanka, the Maldives, Indonesia, Myanmar and Malaysia, demanded to renegotiate some of the expensive infrastructure projects under way in their countries. In response, Beijing has exhibited increased flexibility and responsiveness to the concerns of recipient countries on areas such as debt sustainability and the use of more domestic labour and resources.

While the risk of falling into debt traps is coming to pass in some countries, there are also potential risks to the Chinese economy. Many of the countries to which China is loaning money are far from economically stable and there are fears that if and when they default on the loans, it will crash the Chinese banking system, which would in turn have ripple effects on the broader global economy. There are already signs that China is becoming more aware of this issue. Since 2015, the number of projects being given the go-ahead by the Chinese has declined each year, suggesting that Beijing is placing greater scrutiny on where the money is going.

However, there are still concerns about China's due diligence in assessing the viability of the projects that it's undertaking, leading to fears that many will become white elephants. Again, there are already precedents out there. In Kara-Balta, Kyrgyzstan, the state-owned Zhongda China Petrol company built a US$430 million oil refinery but didn't arrange contracts in advance to supply the

Construction on the US$6 billion Laos–China Railway in 2019. When completed, the railway will stretch for 414 km (257 miles), making it the longest in Asia outside China. There are fears that Laos will be unable to service the debt that it has taken on to pay for the project.

required crude oil, so the refinery is currently running at about six per cent capacity.

And then there's the issue of local corruption – reports have suggested that China expects to lose 80 per cent of its funds in Pakistan, half in Myanmar and a third in Central Asia – and the risk of unmet expectations. It's rare that large infrastructure projects are completed on time and on budget. Most fail to deliver all of the promised benefits and often throw up unexpected environmental and social costs. As more and more BRI projects deliver disappointing results, or fail outright, China could end up suffering significant damage to its reputation.

PHYSICAL BARRIERS, MILITARY AMBITIONS

Another issue that China faces in realising its plans, particularly in Central Asia, is the often-forbidding physical geography. There's a reason why the traders along the ancient Silk Road often transported their goods using yak caravans: Central Asia is home to some of the world's highest mountain ranges and getting from one side to the other means negotiating some extremely high passes. Roads in these regions typically have very short lives, beginning to decay shortly after they are laid. A key question is thus, once the infrastructure has been put in place, who will be responsible for maintaining it?

To complicate matters further, many of these high passes are located in politically unstable regions, which brings security issues into play. The passes themselves are effectively narrow canyons, which makes them extremely vulnerable to military strikes or terrorist attacks.

Indeed, security is a significant consideration. Many of the projects taking place in these politically volatile regions rely on the use of Chinese labour – workers who need to be protected. Already, in Africa and Central and South Asia, Chinese workers have been killed, prompting unusually harsh criticism back in China.

Pakistan is a particularly worrying flashpoint. In August 2018, militants from the Balochistan Liberation Army (BLA), a Pakistani separatist group, attacked a bus carrying Chinese workers to the Saindak mining project in Balochistan. The following November, the group attacked the Chinese consulate in Karachi, killing four people. In May 2019, BLA militants attacked the Pearl Continental Hotel in Gwadar killing five. The next day, the group released a video statement in which it warned China that it faced dire consequences if it didn't pull out of CPEC projects in Balochistan. And in June 2020, four BLA gunmen armed with grenades, automatic rifles and explosives, were killed during an attack on the Pakistan Stock Exchange, along with four security personnel. Pakistan's leading Taliban group, the Tehrik-e-Taliban Pakistan (TTP), has also killed and kidnapped a number of Chinese, mainly in Khyber

Pakhtunkhwa and Balochistan provinces, and security analysts have voiced fears that the group will target projects linked to the BRI in the country's northwest. Anti-China rhetoric regularly appears in TTP and al-Qaeda propaganda.

For China, a potentially welcome side effect of these security issues is that it provides Beijing with an opportunity to realize its global military ambitions. As Chinese companies spread around the world, it presents Beijing with a handy rationale – and in some cases potentially even a need – to broaden its global military capacity in order to safeguard both its investments and the Chinese nationals who are working on them.

However, just such attempts by China to protect its workers and investments have increased geopolitical tensions in some regions. For example, India is particularly opposed to the BRI because of China's investment and engagement in Pakistan. Some of the construction projects related to the CPEC are taking place in parts of Pakistan whose ownership is disputed by India. The Pakistani government has mobilized 15,000 soldiers to protect Chinese workers, including in the disputed regions, inflating the Pakistani military presence there, which hasn't gone down well with the Indian government.

Several other nations, particularly in Western Europe, are also wary of the expansion of Chinese power and influence that BRI represents. In April 2018, ambassadors from 27 of the then 28 EU member states signed a report that was highly critical of the BRI, complaining that it 'runs counter to the EU agenda for liberalizing trade and pushes the balance of power in favour of subsidized Chinese companies'.

The use of Chinese labour has been a particular sore point in many BRI countries. Roughly 90 per cent of BRI projects are being carried out exclusively by Chinese firms employing Chinese labour. At the end of 2018, there were just over 200,000 Chinese workers in Africa alone, down from a high of more than 263,000 in 2015. This has stoked resentment among local populations, who will have been hoping, and were more than likely promised, that the projects would boost employment. In some cases, this has led to violent protests.

ANY PORT IN A STORM

Concerns that China's development rhetoric is disguising ulterior motives are at their most acute when it comes to the port deals that it has pursued around the Indian Ocean. In recent years, Chinese firms – both state-owned and politically linked private companies – have acquired 15 ports across the Indian Ocean region, in countries including Thailand, Cambodia, Indonesia, Myanmar, Sri Lanka, Pakistan and Djibouti, the site of China's first formal overseas military base. But while Beijing has characterized the deals as commercial propositions that will update infrastructure and stimulate trade, according to a report released by US research NGO C4ADS, a primary driver for the acquisitions is to give China's navy the option of logistical support. Under Chinese law, all Chinese transportation firms must, if called upon, provide support for military missions.

The report states that Chinese analysts, particularly those with military backgrounds, describe the port investments as 'discreetly enabling China to enhance its military presence in the Indo-Pacific'. By setting up a network of Chinese-controlled ports, Beijing is enabling the Chinese navy to operate more widely, in much the same way as coaling stations set up by the Dutch, British and US navies did during the 19th century.

China's actions are particularly ringing alarm bells in the USA and India. The former was already concerned about China's aggressive expansion into the South China Sea, while the latter was worried that the BRI is a smokescreen behind which China will attempt to seize strategic control of the Indian Ocean, worries that can only have been deepened by the fact that it has now effectively been 'fenced in' by Chinese-controlled ports at the top of the Bay of Bengal, in Sri Lanka and in Pakistan.

THE DIGITAL SILK ROAD

Chinese ambitions have also moved firmly into the digital sphere. First announced in 2015 in a government white paper, the Digital Silk Road is, like the BRI, a relatively loose umbrella label that covers a wide range of foreign and domestic policy objectives. Broadly speaking, the plan is to bring advanced digital infrastructure, such as broadband and mobile-phone networks, e-commerce hubs and smart ports and cities, to BRI countries in order to support the overarching BRI strategy. Beijing is keen to enhance digital connectivity along the BRI trade corridors while simultaneously extending its political influence, exporting its industrial overcapacity, helping to facilitate the global expansion of Chinese businesses and generally furthering its ascendance as a technological superpower.

Like the BRI, the DSR is loosely defined – less a clearly delineated set of projects than a 'brand' for virtually any telecommunications- or data-related product sales or business activities by China-based tech companies. There is limited central coordination at the working level, with the state generally not involved in day-to-day DSR operations. Instead, implementation of the plan is decentralized, with Beijing only choosing to intervene when it sees an opportunity to advance its wider strategic objectives.

In May 2017, at the inaugural BRI forum in Beijing, President Xi reiterated his desire to use technological development to support the development of the BRI. He called for further integration of 'frontier areas' such as the digital economy, artificial intelligence, nanotechnology and quantum computing, as well as big data, cloud computing and smart cities into the BRI. The second BRI Forum, held in April 2019, featured a separate session on the DSR, attended by almost 30 countries. At the forum, official state media claimed that the DSR 'not only promotes the development of the digital service sector, such as cross-border e-commerce, smart cities, telemedicine and internet finance, but also accelerates technological progress including computing, big data, Internet of Things, artificial intelligence, blockchain and quantum computing.'

At the event, Beijing signed cooperation agreements with at least 22 countries, including Japan, New Zealand, Israel, Austria, Chile, Brazil, Indonesia, Pakistan and Kenya.

Among the companies leading the DSR charge is the Chinese tech giant Huawei, which has now signed contracts with 28 countries in Europe alone relating to 5G network roll-outs. Huawei has also been in talks with several nations in Central and Southeast Asia, Africa and elsewhere about smart city projects – or as it prefers to call them, 'safe city' solutions – that use Chinese AI and networked surveillance cameras to improve public security. In April 2019, the company signed a US$175 million contract with the Kenyan government, funded with Chinese concessional loans, to provide support for the Konza Data Centre and Smart Cities project, a planned technology hub located 65 km (40 miles) south of the Kenyan capital. Pakistan has also signed a deal with the Chinese government that extended a US$124 million concessional loan to be spent on Huawei technology as part of a safe city project in Islamabad.

While the DSR plan is primarily focused on overseas development, there is also a domestic element, focused on the development of advanced technologies that will support China's global economic and military power, including satellite-navigation systems, artificial intelligence and quantum computing. And despite the chaos and economic slowdown caused by the spread of Covid-19, the Communist Party has been calling for an expansion of domestic 5G investments. In response, China's three state-owned telecom operators, China Mobile, China Unicom and China Telecom, have stepped up their efforts to roll out a functional (if limited) 5G network across the country. By the end of the year, they hope to have built 550,000 new base stations, with coverage expanding from 50 cities in 2019 to an estimated 300 cities. The three companies have also announced plans to create a new 5G messaging service in direct competition with the existing domestic social-messaging platforms, such as WeChat and QQ.

However, the DSR initiative has mainly been framed as a way for China to help developing countries bridge the digital divide

Huawei demonstrates its 'safe city' technology at an event in Moscow in 2018.

and bring their digital infrastructure up to developed-world standards, in the process paving the way for programs to develop online education, smart working and remote health services. Chinese firms are then ready and waiting to provide those sorts of programs. For example, in 2017, the African Union launched its Smart Health Monitoring Room using ZTE technology and hospitals in several countries, including Italy and Poland, are now using AI-enabled Covid-19 diagnostic systems that were developed by Chinese companies.

There is a vast untapped market for China to target – almost half the global population still lacks access to the internet – and one of the DSR's key thrusts has been to support the expansion of Chinese companies such as Huawei, China Mobile, China Telecom, China Unicom Alibaba, Tencent and Baidu into emerging markets, using the market access afforded by BRI projects to compete with leading US and European companies.

Some of the projects under the DSR umbrella have received heavy state backing. Huawei and its rival, ZTE, have used multi-billion-pound Chinese government loans to finance the construction of much of Africa's digital infrastructure. In 2015 and 2017, the Chinese government loaned more money for African information and communications technology infrastructure development than came from African governments, multilateral agencies and the G7 nations combined. Many other projects are operating without state funding, but Chinese tech executives are still keen to self-brand their international activities as being part of the DSR as a way of currying favour with the government and perhaps bringing political or, eventually, financial support.

IMPROVING DIGITAL CONNECTIVITY

One of the key parts of the DSR plan is the improvement of digital connectivity by rolling out fibre-optic cables. The availability of advanced fibre-optic cables is vital for the viability of 5G networks, so their roll-out has been prioritized by Beijing. Through its tech corporations, notably Huawei and ZTE, China can deliver high-quality submarine and terrestrial fibre-optic cables considerably more cheaply than their European and US competitors. In Asia, China owns or has assisted in the building of about 30 per cent of existing cables and 54 per cent of planned cables; globally it owns or supplies 11 per cent of existing cables and 24 per cent of planned cables.

These types of projects can act as 'easy wins' for China. While the large infrastructure projects taking place along the CPEC are mired in delays, Huawei has laid an 820-km (510 mile) fibre-optic cable that runs across the border and deep into Pakistan. The project, which was 85 per cent funded by China Eximbank, took less than two years and cost only US$44 million, less than the cost of 4 km (2.5 miles) of railway in Pakistan.

One of the larger projects currently under way is the Pakistan and East Africa Connecting Europe cable (formerly the Pakistan East Africa Cable Express; PEACE). Being built by Chinese companies, including Huawei Marine and the Hengtong Group, with part funding from the state-owned China Construction Bank, the high-speed fibre-optic cable is set to span some 15,000 kilometres (9,320 miles), offering the shortest routes from China to Europe and Africa, and dramatically reducing latency. Beginning in Pakistan at Gwadar Port, a key node in the CPEC, it will run south to Djibouti, where China has constructed its first overseas military base, Somalia, Kenya, South Africa and the Seychelles, and north to Egypt and on to France, a hub for Europe's submarine cable networks.

Chinese companies such as Alibaba Cloud, Daily Tech and Global Switch are also busy building data centres along the BRI to help facilitate the expansion of cloud-computing services and extend the reach of telecoms companies such as China Telecom Global. This has been taking place in tandem with increasing Chinese investments in companies offering digital services – from ride-hailing to financial technology – along BRI routes.

North Africa is one region that has significant Chinese tech-sector activity. All of the countries in the region have signed up to the BRI and the region is home to several large infrastructural projects, including the upgrade of Morocco's Tangier Med Port, the largest port on the Mediterranean, and Egypt's new administrative capital. These are now being followed by a number of ICT projects. For example, in February 2019, Huawei opened a cloud data centre in Egypt, its first in the region. The company has also signed a contract to build a data centre for the Algerian customs agency.

China's largest investment project in North Africa is Tangier Tech, an ambitious US$11 billion smart city development in northern Morocco being developed by China Communication Construction Company and China Road and its subsidiary, China Road and Bridge Corp. Announced in March 2017, the 2,000-hectare (4,942 acre) city will act as an industrial and financial hub with connections to rail and motorway networks, and Tangier Med Port. It's projected to create 100,000 jobs and house 300,000 people; some 200 Chinese companies, many of them part of the tech industry, have already agreed to open offices in the new city.

THE SPACE SILK ROAD

As if opening up new overland, maritime and digital Silk Roads wasn't enough, the Chinese government has also added space to its grand plans. The Spatial Information Corridor (SIC) project aims to augment the economic development created by the BRI by offering new services related to satellite technology, including communications, remote sensing and navigation. The Chinese government considers the development of space technology to be essential for driving the BRI forward. And as with the BRI and DSR, the SIC forms part of Beijing's quest for China to be viewed as a global leader.

Central to the plans is China's BeiDou Navigation Satellite System, which is designed to replace the US-operated GPS system and the EU's Galileo system, giving the Chinese military and government full independence from foreign-run satellite positioning technology. In June 2020, China successfully deployed the system's final satellite, bringing the total to 35 (GPS uses 24). Already, about 120 countries are using BeiDou's services for port traffic monitoring and other services. In addition to its primary role in providing positioning information, BeiDou is also seen as a vehicle for promoting the export of Chinese-made mobile phones and software applications that use the system.

Satellite technology is also playing a direct role in several BRI infrastructure projects. For example, Hong Kong-based operator APT Satellite is working with a Chinese state-owned company that's constructing railways in Laos and Thailand, using its satellites to open up communication channels with the company's headquarters in China.

The development of satellite technology also gives China the opportunity to present itself as a benevolent member of the global community. The China National Space Administration has touted

A rocket carrying the final BeiDou satellite launches on 23 June 2020. The BeiDou system is intended to provide a Chinese alternative to GPS.

the SIC's potential to boost capacity-building in developing countries in line with the UN's Sustainable Development Goals. And in May 2020, the China Meteorological Administration announced that countries involved in the BRI would be able to access high-frequency data from China's Fengyun meteorological satellites to help deal with meteorological disasters such as typhoons, severe rainstorms, wildfires and sandstorms. Such timely and accurate information would potentially be a boon for national authorities working to prevent disasters or attempting to provide disaster relief, particularly in countries that currently don't have access to such information.

By bringing space-related commerce under the BRI umbrella, Beijing is also helping Chinese satellite companies to sell their products to countries that are already making infrastructure investments under the initiative. Among the deals that have already been struck, the state-owned satellite manufacturer China Great Wall Industry (CGWIC) is building two communication satellites for Nigeria, with financing provided by China in exchange for an equity stake. It has also signed a deal to build and launch a communications satellite for Cambodia. And in May 2018, CGWIC worked with APT Satellite to launch a satellite to provide telecommunication and broadcast services for a number of BRI countries, including Mongolia and Myanmar.

GROWING FEARS

Like the BRI, the DSR has raised fears about China's motives and behaviour. Although many of these fears are probably overstated, others are already being realized.

While China pushes its line that the DSR is all about improving digital connectivity in developing economies, in the West, many see it as a back door for spying and a vehicle for spreading authoritarianism and curbing human rights. There are also fears that by dominating the digital landscape in the developing world, China will hinder the ability of local companies to compete.

In particular, the geopolitical posturing between China and the USA over global technology development – characterized as a digital arms race or a technology cold war – has gone up several levels. The US government has recently put pressure on other Western governments to shut Chinese firms out of their critical digital infrastructure – in particular their new 5G networks – citing military and security risks associated with the use of Chinese technology. Its efforts have been only partially successful: Romania, Poland, the Czech Republic, Latvia, Estonia, the UK, Australia, New Zealand, India and Japan have banned Chinese corporations from participation in the development of their 5G mobile phone networks, while France has said that it will severely limit the use of Chinese technology in its own networks. However, Ireland, Spain, Austria, Hungary, Germany and Sweden are still working with Huawei to develop their networks. The USA's efforts have been hampered by the fact that Huawei's 5G is both more advanced and cheaper than other networks.

There are also fears that China will use its control of internet operations, whether through terrestrial fibre-optic cables or satellites, to monitor data flows for business and intelligence operations. In January 2018, African Union (AU) officials accused China of diverting confidential data from its Chinese-built headquarters in Ethiopia to Shanghai every night between 2012 and 2017. In the aftermath, the AU replaced its servers and declined China's offer to configure them.

Control of data flows will also potentially enable Chinese intelligence agents to track and target individuals, and to manipulate and disrupt information flows, by cutting off access to the internet, for example. And it could also help Chinese technology companies improve their applications and algorithms, and gain significant insights into local markets, giving them a competitive edge over local competitors.

DIGITAL AUTHORITARIANISM

Concerns have also been raised that the DSR is being used by China to export its 'digital-authoritarian' model to countries along the BRI. Access to the internet is severely curtailed in China through the so-called Great Firewall and the government is also increasingly using facial recognition technology for the surveillance of its population, particularly in Xinjiang. These sorts of techniques for population control are likely to be very appealing to other authoritarian regimes, many of whom are already involved in the BRI, and China has been actively marketing them in the developing world, particularly in Africa. Since early in 2017, China has hosted seminars on cyberspace management with representatives from 36 countries. In Vietnam, Uganda, Tanzania and elsewhere, these discussions were followed by the implementation of restrictive new cybersecurity measures that resemble those in China. Intelligence officials from several African nations have also had meetings with Huawei in Shenzhen, accompanied by Chinese government officials.

While the Chinese government provides training and advice on policies, legislation and other techniques of population control, Chinese companies provide the necessary technological infrastructure. According to Freedom House, Chinese firms have provided or are set to provide internet infrastructure to at least 38 countries and artificial intelligence systems for use in law enforcement to 18 countries. In North Africa, a number of telecoms operators are installing Chinese digital surveillance tools, and since September 2018, Huawei has been working with the Serbian government on a surveillance project in the capital, Belgrade. It has also been suggested that the hosting platforms being installed by Chinese companies in some parts of the world come with full internet shutdown options pre-installed.

In Uganda, the president, Yoweri Museveni, is alleged to have worked with Huawei to decrypt the communications of his political rival, resulting in a series of arrests; and Huawei has also been accused of assisting the Zambian government with the surveillance of political opponents (both claims have been denied by Huawei and the governments involved). And in 2017, reports emerged that the state-owned China National Electronics Import and Export Corporation (CEIEC) was selling Uganda 'a comprehensive cybersecurity solution, including technical capacity to monitor and prevent social media abuse'.

Egypt is also drawing heavily on China's model of internet governance. A new cybercrime law passed in 2018 places significant constraints on citizens' rights in the name of national security and the Egyptian government has blocked access to hundreds of websites, primarily those belonging to media organizations. In April 2019, Egypt signed a memorandum of agreement with several Chinese tech firms to further deepen cooperation in areas including artificial intelligence, cloud computing and surveillance systems.

Chinese companies such as CloudWalk, Hikvision and Yitsu have provided technological assistance to governments keen to create artificial intelligence and facial recognition systems capable of identifying what they consider to be threats to public order. In Zimbabwe, for example, the government is working with CloudWalk to create a national facial recognition and monitoring system that will be placed in larger cities and public transport stations. While governments state that these systems are being implemented in order to reduce crime, there are concerns that they will be used to target political opponents. Meanwhile, for the Chinese companies involved, these deals offer a wealth of data for fine-tuning their software systems, potentially giving them a significant commercial advantage.

There are also concerns that Chinese companies are using consumer applications, including social media apps such as TikTok and Virtual Private Network apps, to harvest potentially sensitive user data. As users often turn to applications such as these during times of political instability, observers are also concerned that the potential exists for China to interfere in democratic processes. Such fears are in the process of being acted upon by the US government, which in September 2020 attempted to shut down domestic access to TikTok and WeChat.

Concerns about data harvesting were given fresh impetus that same month when a dataset compiled by Chinese tech company Zhenhua Data that contained the personal details of millions of people from around the world – including British prime minister Boris Johnson, the British royal family and military figures – was leaked to a US academic. The company has been linked to China's military and intelligence networks, and there are suggestions that the data was intended for use in monitoring critics of China and exerting influence.

China's increasing dominance of the global communication market will also improve its ability to shape governance of the digital realm – potentially in ways that normalize censorship and otherwise restrict online freedoms – as well as aligning global technology standards with proprietary technologies used by Chinese suppliers. China has reportedly mobilized significant resources to influence the setting of technical standards by the International Telecommunication Union, the UN agency responsible for information and communication technologies.

There are rumours that Chinese officials offered business deals to foreign companies in exchange for their support for Chinese technical proposals. If enough countries are already using Chinese-style internet restrictions and Chinese-made technology, it makes it easier for China to shape governance in these realms and give Chinese firms an advantage over competitors also working to meet demand.

COVID-19 AND THE BRI

The emergence of the novel coronavirus that causes Covid-19 in the Chinese city of Wuhan at the end of 2019 quickly threw plans for the BRI into disarray. Restrictions on travel of workers and disrupted logistics and supply chains caused by the closing of borders and economic shutdowns designed to contain the new virus caused numerous projects to be halted. According to a survey carried out by the Chinese Ministry of Foreign Affairs in June, about a fifth of BRI projects had been 'seriously affected' by the pandemic, with a further 30–40 per cent 'somewhat affected'. China had not heard of any major projects being cancelled.

In many cases, however, the shutdowns were short-lived. Work on the new US$6 billion China–Laos railway, for example, stopped for just 23 days. Construction was put on hold on 1 April 2020 when the Lao government closed its borders in response to the pandemic, but by the end of May, Chinese workers and engineers were back at the site, although in reduced numbers and only after undergoing quarantine.

Of more concern to Beijing is the wider economic impact of the virus. Many of the countries to which it has loaned funds have seen their economies contract significantly – largely due to sharp falls in commodity prices, a reduction in demand for those commodities and a drop in the value of remittances from migrant labourers – raising the risk of more loan defaults. The G20 responded to the global economic slowdown by agreeing to suspend debt payments for low-income countries. China backed this agreement and later announced a freeze on debt repayments for 77 developing countries until the end of 2020.

The impact of the pandemic is also making foreign governments understandably wary of economic risks, slowing the take-up of BRI projects and the associated Chinese debt. Many of China's partners are also being forced to review the viability of the BRI projects to which they've committed, which could lead to renegotiations or even project cancellations.

However, the impact of the virus has also opened up new opportunities. For example, the significant drop in international flights and disruption of cargo shipping saw a large increase in the volume of rail freight along the BRI route between Asia and Europe, with record numbers of trains passing through Duisburg, a key German hub for services to and from China. Although some train services were halted during the height of the outbreak, most were quickly restored and some operators even opened new routes to take advantage of the slowdown in air and sea freight.

The spread of Covid-19 has also opened up new opportunities for the DSR. Widespread lockdowns forced a significant increase in remote working, underscoring the importance of digital connectivity. The pandemic has also enabled Chinese tech companies to pitch their products as ways to improve the response to the current outbreak and help to prevent future pandemics. For example, surveillance companies have introduced thermal-imaging systems to detect fevers; Alibaba and Tencent have released apps that generate QR codes that provide information about whether the user poses a health risk; and Alibaba has offered its cloud services for those attempting to model outbreaks and for connecting health professionals to each other. While these sorts of systems are also offered by Western companies, the Chinese versions often come with fewer privacy protections.

And there are signs that Beijing is attempting to take advantage of the opportunities generated by the pandemic to play a 'saviour role'; China's state-owned media has already released numerous articles framing the BRI as a means to jumpstart a global economic recovery in the wake of the pandemic shutdowns and Beijing has been making highly conspicuous displays of aid to other countries struggling to cope with the effects of the pandemic.

Nowhere is the adoption of this saviour rhetoric more obvious than in healthcare. Beijing's provision of medical assistance and supplies to countries around the world, particularly those that are part of the BRI, is helping to draw attention away from the fact that China was the initial source of the novel coronavirus, and that its early response to the disease was poorly managed. But it is also helping China to position itself as a global health leader. Chinese embassies have been providing medical aid and consultation, while medical supplies have been provided by companies working on BRI projects, such as Huawei and the China Communications Construction Company.

THE HEALTH SILK ROAD

The pandemic has also seen President Xi revive his idea of developing a 'Health Silk Road' (HSR). In March 2020, during a phone conversation with Italian Prime Minister Giuseppe Conte about the supply of medical teams and supplies, Xi raised the possibility of working with Italy to build an HSR. The term quickly began to gain traction among Chinese officials and state media outlets, who characterized it as an effort to improve the governance of global public health.

Effectively a rhetorical extension of the BRI into the healthcare arena, in much the same way as the DSR has moved it into the technological sphere, the HSR is, like both the BRI and the DSR, a vague umbrella term for any healthcare-related activities carried out by the Chinese state or Chinese companies. It was first used by Xi during a visit to Geneva in January 2017, during which he signed a memorandum of understanding with the World Health Organization that committed to the construction of an HSR designed to improve public health in countries along the BRI.

The Covid-19 pandemic offered Xi a perfect excuse to reinvigorate the concept and many of the health-related projects mentioned previously in the discussion of the DSR will undoubtedly form part of the HSR. The pandemic-enforced slowdown of many BRI projects will also likely see more announcements relating to the HSR in order to foster a perception of continued progress. And by grouping together Chinese healthcare projects under the HSR banner, Beijing will surely be hoping to highlight the contrasting responses of China and the West – and the USA in particular – to the pandemic, and position China as a global healthcare leader.

A NEW GOLDEN ERA?

While there is a general lack of clarity surrounding both the BRI and DSR, one thing is clear: China is locked in to the initiatives for the foreseeable future. Xi is firmly ensconced as the Chinese leader and the BRI is his signature foreign-policy project, to the point where it has even been written into the Chinese constitution. Without a very significant shake-up of the Chinese leadership, or a significant collapse of the Chinese economy, it's unlikely that the BRI will be going away any time soon.

— Bibliography —

Barisitz, Stephan: *Central Asia and the Silk Road: Economic Rise and Decline over Several Millennia*, Springer, Cham, 2017

Beckwith, Christopher I. *Empires of the Silk Road: A History of Central Eurasia from the Bronze Age to the Present*, Princeton University Press, Princeton, 2009

Benjamin, Craig: *The Yuezhi: Origin, Migration and the Conquest of Northern Bactria*, Brepols, Turnhout, 2007

Boulnois, Luce: *Silk Road: Monks, Warriors and Merchants*, Odyssey Books, Hong Kong, 2003

Di Cosmo, Nicola: *Ancient China and its Enemies: The Rise of Nomadic Power in East Asian History*, Cambridge University Press, Cambridge, 2002

Elisseeff, Vadime (Ed.): *The Silk Roads: Highways of Culture and Commerce*, Berghahn Books, New York, 2000

Elverskog, Johan: *Buddhism and Islam on the Silk Road*, University of Pennsylvania Press, Philadelphia, 2013

Frankopan, Peter: *The Silk Roads: A New History of the World*, Bloomsbury, London, 2015

Hansen, Valerie: *The Silk Road: A New History*, Oxford University Press, Oxford, 2015

Hedin, Sven: *Through Asia*, Harper and Brothers, London, 1899

Hedin, Sven: *Central Asia and Tibet*, Hurst and Blackett, London, 1903

Hedin, Sven: *My Life as an Explorer*, National Geographic, Washington D.C., 2003

Hedin, Sven: *The Silk Road*, Tauris Parke, London, 2009

Hopkirk, Peter: *Foreign Devils on the Silk Road: The Search for the Lost Treasures of Central Asia*, John Murray, London, 1980

Knobloch, Edgar: *Treasures of the Great Silk Road*, The History

Press, Stroud, 2013

Kuzmina, E. E.: *The Prehistory of the Silk Road*, University of Pennsylvania Press, Philadelphia, 2008

Liu, Xinru: *The Silk Road in World History*, Oxford University Press, Oxford, 2010

Liu, Xinru: *The Silk Roads: A Brief History with Documents*, Palgrave Macmillan, Basingstoke, 2012

Mair, Victor H. & Hickman, Jane (Eds.): *Reconfiguring the Silk Road: New Research on East-West Exchange in Antiquity*. University of Pennsylvania Museum of Archaeology and Anthropolgy, Philadelphia, 2014

McLaughlin, Raoul: *The Roman Empire and the Silk Routes: The Ancient World Economy and the Empires of Parthia, Central Asia and Han China*, Pen & Sword History, Barnsley, 2016

Miksic, John N.: *Singapore and the Silk Road of the Sea, 1300–1800*, NUS Press, Singapore, 2014

Millard, James A.: *The Silk Road: A Very Short Introduction*, Oxford University Press, Oxford, 2013

Miller, Tom: *China's Asian Dream: Empire Building along the New Silk Road*, Zed Books, London, 2017

Morgan, Joyce & Walters, Conrad. *Journeys on the Silk Road: A Desert Explorer, Buddha's Secret Library, and the Unearthing of the World's Oldest Printed Book*, Lyons Press, Guilford 2012

Stein, Aurel: *Innermost Asia: Detailed Report of Explorations in Central Asia, Kansu and Eastern Iran*, Clarendon Press, Oxford, 1928

Stein, Aurel: *Ruins of Desert Cathay: Personal Narrative of Explorations in Central Asia and Westernmost China*, B. Blom, New York, 1968

Stein, Aurel: *On Ancient Central-Asian Tracks: Brief Narrative of Three Expeditions in Innermost Asia and North-western China*, Macmillan and Co., London, 1933

Vainker, Shelagh: *Chinese Silk: A Cultural History*, British Museum Press, London, 2004

Von Le Coq, Albert: *Buried Treasures of Chinese Turkestan*, Oxford University Press (China), Hong Kong, 1985

Whitfield, Roderick: *Cave Temples of Mogao at Dunhuang: Art and History on the Silk Road*, Getty Publications, Los Angeles, 2015

Whitfield, Susan: *Life along the Silk Road*, John Murray, London, 1999

Whitfield, Susan (Ed.): *The Silk Road: Trade, Travel, War and Faith*, Serindia, Chicago, 2004

Whitfield, Susan: *Silk, Slaves, and Stupas: Material Culture of the Silk Road*, University of California Press, Berkeley, 2018

Wood, Frances: *The Silk Road: Two Thousand Years in the Heart of Asia*, British Library Publishing Division, London, 2004

Wriggins, Sally Hovey: *The Silk Road Journey with Xuanzang*, Westview Press, Boulder, 2004

— INDEX —